Infographica

Infogr

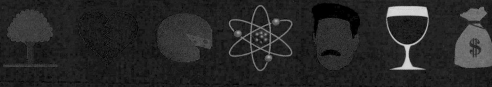

aphica

Martin & Simon Toseland

Quercus

Contents

The league of chilies

Chili heat is measured on the Scoville Scale, which is based on the number of drops of water required to make the taste of chili undetectable. The measurement is expressed in SHU (Scoville Heat Units) and ranges from the innocuous bell pepper to the eyewatering, ambulance-calling Trinidad Moruga Scorpion

Bell pepper
0 (no heat)

Pimento, pepperoncini
1–500

Anaheim, poblano, rocotillo
500–2,500

Jalapeño, guajillo, New Mexican Anaheim, paprika
2,500–8,000

Serrano, some chipotle
10,000–23,000

Cayenne, ají, tabasco, some chipotle
30,000–50,000

Thai, malagueta, chiltepin, pequin
50,000–100,000

Some habanero, Scotch bonnet, datil, rocoto, Jamaican hot, African Thai
100,000–350,000

Red savina, some habanero
350,000–580,000

Naga jolokia
855,000–1,050,000

Dorset Naga (used in one of the world's hottest curries "The Bombay Burner")
1,032,310

Infinity chilli
1,067,286

Naga viper
1,382,118

Trinidad Moruga Scorpion—current world record holder
2,009,231

Law-enforcement grade pepper spray used for crowd control is usually 1,500,000–2,000,000 SHU

Faster than the speed of sound

Some of the fastest speed records from 1899 to the present

124.2mph / 200kph

248.5mph / 400kph

372.8mph / 600k

372.8mph / 600kph Golden Arrow, March 11 1929

334kph Sunbeam, March 29 1927

372.3kph Triplex, April 22 1928

328kph Babs, April 28 1926

275.2kph Duesenburg, April 27 1920

251.1kph Packard, February 17 1919

241.2kph Benz, April 23 1911

228.1kph Stanley, January 23 1906

231.4mph /

207.6mph /

203.8mph /

156mph /

171mph /

149.9mph /

141.7mph / 195.7kph Darracq, December 30 1905

121.6mph / 176.4kph Napier, January 25 1905

109.6mph / 168.4kph Gobron-Brillié, July 21 1904

104.7mph / 166.7kph Mercedes, May 25 1904

103.6mph / 156.5kph Ford, January 12 1904

97.3mph / 147kph Mors, November 17 1902

91.4mph / 124.1kph Serpollet, April 13 1902

77.1mph / 120.8kph Jenatzy, April 29 1899

75.1mph / 105.9kph Jeantaud, March 4 1899

65.8mph /

57.7mph / 92.8kph

8

766.6mph / 1,233.7kph
Thrust SSC. October 15 1997

622.4mph / 1,001.7kph Blue Flame,
October 23 1970

600.6mph / 966.6kph Spirit of America Sonic 1,
November 15 1965

576.6mph / 927.9kph Green Monster, November 7 1965

526.3mph / 847kph Spirit of America, October 15 1964

497mph / 800kph

621.3mph / 1,000kph

413.2mph / 665kph Wingfoot Express, October 5 1964

745.5mph / 1,200kph

394.2mph / 634.4kph Railton, September 16 1947

357.5mph / 575.3kph Thunderbolt, September 16 1938

301.1mph / 484.6kph Bluebird, September 3 1935

Closer to God

The tallest religious statue by country

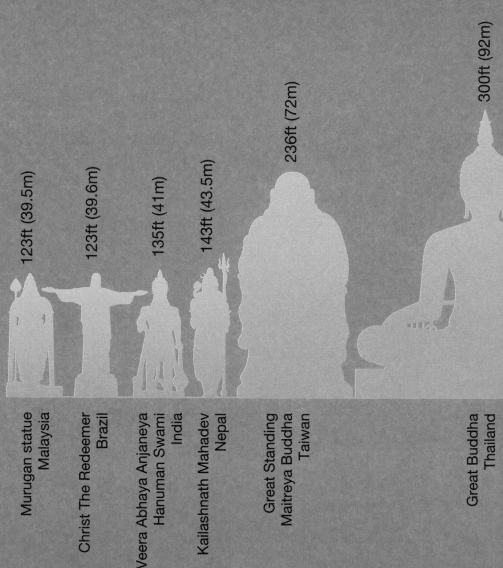

123ft (39.5m) — Murugan statue, Malaysia

123ft (39.6m) — Christ The Redeemer, Brazil

135ft (41m) — Veera Abhaya Anjaneya Hanuman Swami, India

143ft (43.5m) — Kailashnath Mahadev, Nepal

236ft (72m) — Great Standing Maitreya Buddha, Taiwan

300ft (92m) — Great Buddha, Thailand

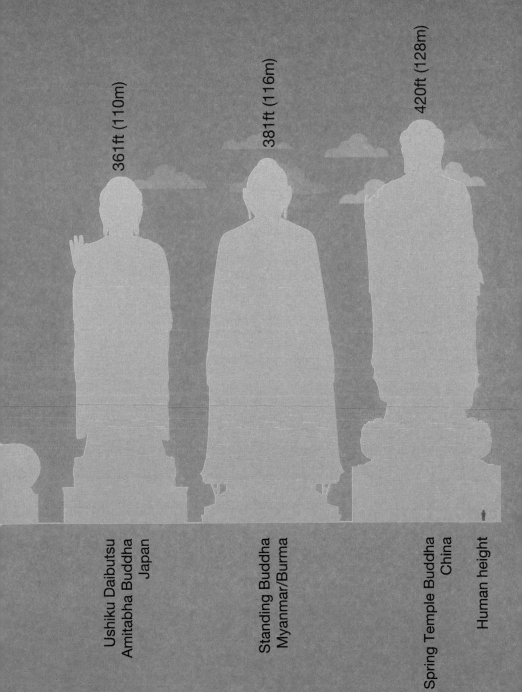

361ft (110m) — Ushiku Daibutsu Amitabha Buddha Japan

381ft (116m) — Standing Buddha Myanmar/Burma

420ft (128m) — Spring Temple Buddha China

Human height

Bottling it

The world's most expensive wine at auction—measured by cost (in USD) per 4 ounce glass—and date of auction

A 1787 Chateau Margaux was valued in 1989 at $500,000 by its owner, New York wine merchant William Sokolin. He planned to open it at a dinner at the Four Seasons Hotel. Sadly, he never got to taste the wine—a waiter knocked over the bottle, which shattered on the floor.

His insurance company paid out $225,000 ($411,269 adjusted for inflation) or a staggering $68,544 per glass (today's prices).

Chateau Lafitte 1787

$52,500
1985

Chateau Yquem 1787

$19,500
2011

Chateau Yquem 1787

$16,667
2006

Screaming Eagle Cabernet 1992

$10,417
2000

Massandra 1775

$8,667
2001

Chateau Mouton-Rothschild 1945

$7,833
2007

Penfolds Grange Hermltage 1951

$7,663
2004

Cheval Blanc 1947

$6,329
2006

Royal DeMaria 2000

$5,167
2006

Chateau Mouton-Rothschild 1945

$5,000
2006

Montrachet 1978 Domaine de la Romanée-Conti

$4,750
2001

Chateau Mouton-Rothschild 1945

$3,833
1997

13

Nobel writers

The winners of the Nobel Prize for Literature, grouped by the age they were when they won

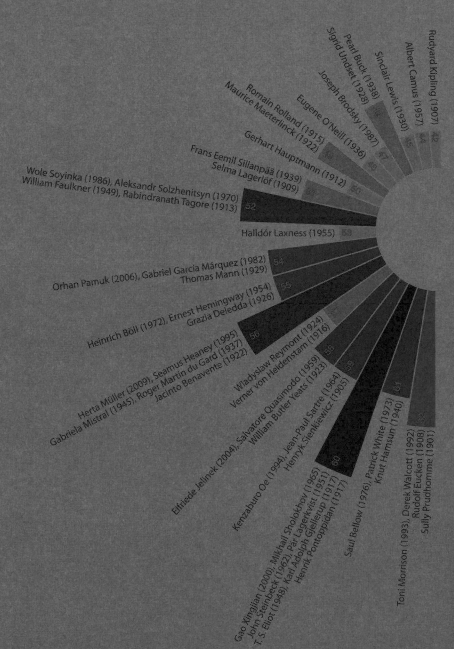

Rudyard Kipling (1907)
Albert Camus (1957)
Sinclair Lewis (1930)
Joseph Brodsky (1987)
Pearl Buck (1938)
Sigrid Undset (1928)
Eugene O'Neill (1936)
Romain Rolland (1915)
Maurice Maeterlinck (1922)
Gerhart Hauptmann (1912)
Frans Eemil Sillanpää (1939)
Selma Lagerlöf (1909)

Wole Soyinka (1986), Aleksandr Solzhenitsyn (1970)
William Faulkner (1949), Rabindranath Tagore (1913)

Halldór Laxness (1955)

Orhan Pamuk (2006), Gabriel García Márquez (1982)
Thomas Mann (1929)

Heinrich Böll (1972), Ernest Hemingway (1954)
Grazia Deledda (1926)

Herta Müller (2009), Seamus Heaney (1995)
Gabriela Mistral (1945), Roger Martin du Gard (1937)
Jacinto Benavente (1922)

Wladyslaw Reymont (1924)
Verner von Heidenstam (1916)

Elfriede Jelinek (2004), Salvatore Quasimodo (1959)
William Butler Yeats (1923)

Kenzaburo Oe (1994), Jean-Paul Sartre (1964)
Henryk Sienkiewicz (1905)

Gao Xingjian (2000), Mikhail Sholokhov (1965)
John Steinbeck (1962), Pär Lagerkvist (1951)
T. S. Eliot (1948), Karl Adolph Gjellerup (1917)
Henrik Pontoppidan (1917)

Saul Bellow (1976), Patrick White (1973)
Knut Hamsun (1940)

Toni Morrison (1993), Derek Walcott (1992)
Rudolf Eucken (1908)
Sully Prudhomme (1901)

42
44
45
47
48
49
50
51
52
53
54
55
56
57
58
59
60
61
62

14

John M. Coetzee (2003), Samuel Beckett (1969)
Giorgos Seferis (1963), Ivan Bunin (1933)

John Galsworthy (1932)

Pablo Neruda (1971), François Mauriac (1952)
Luigi Pirandello (1934), Erik Axel Karlfeldt (1931)

Jean-Marie Gustave Le Clézio (2008),Nadine Gordimer (1991)
Odysseus Elytis (1979), Miguel Ángel Asturias (1967)
Boris Pasternak (1958), Henri Bergson (1927)

Sir V. S. Naipaul (2001), Czesław Miłosz (1980)
Yasunari Kawabata (1968), Ivo Andrić (1961)
Hermann Hesse (1946), George Bernard Shaw (1925)

Harry Martinson (1974)

Dario Fo (1997), Johannes Vilhelm Jensen (1944)
Giosuè Carducci (1906), Bjørnstjerne Bjørnson (1903)

Günter Grass (1999), Claude Simon (1985)
William Golding (1983), José Echegaray (1904)

Imre Kertész (2002), Wisława Szymborska (1996)
Camilo José Cela (1989), Saint-John Perse (1960)

Mario Vargas Llosa (2010), Isaac Bashevis Singer (1978)
Eyvind Johnson (1974), Carl Friedrich
Georg Spitteler (1919), Frédéric Mistral (1904)

Harold Pinter (2005), Nelly Sachs (1966)
Juan Ramón Jiménez (1956)

José Saramago (1998), Octavio Paz (1990)
Elias Canetti (1981)

Naguib Mahfouz (1988), Anatole France (1921)

Shmuel Yosef Agnon (1966)
Bertrand Russell (1950)
André Gide (1947)
Vicente Alexandre (1977), Eugenio Montale (1975)
Sir Winston Churchill (1953)

Tomas Tranströmer (1972)
Paul Heyse (1910)

Jaroslav Seifert (1984)

Theodor Mommsen (1902)

Doris Lessing (2007)

15

Better than receiving?

The top 20 countries in terms of charitable donations according to the World Giving Index. The percentage score is based on money given, volunteering time, and help given to a stranger

Guyana 45%

Malta 45%

Qatar 45%

Denmark 46%

Iceland 47%

Liberia 47%

Nigeria 47%

Turkmenistan 47%

Morocco 48%

Hong Kong 49%

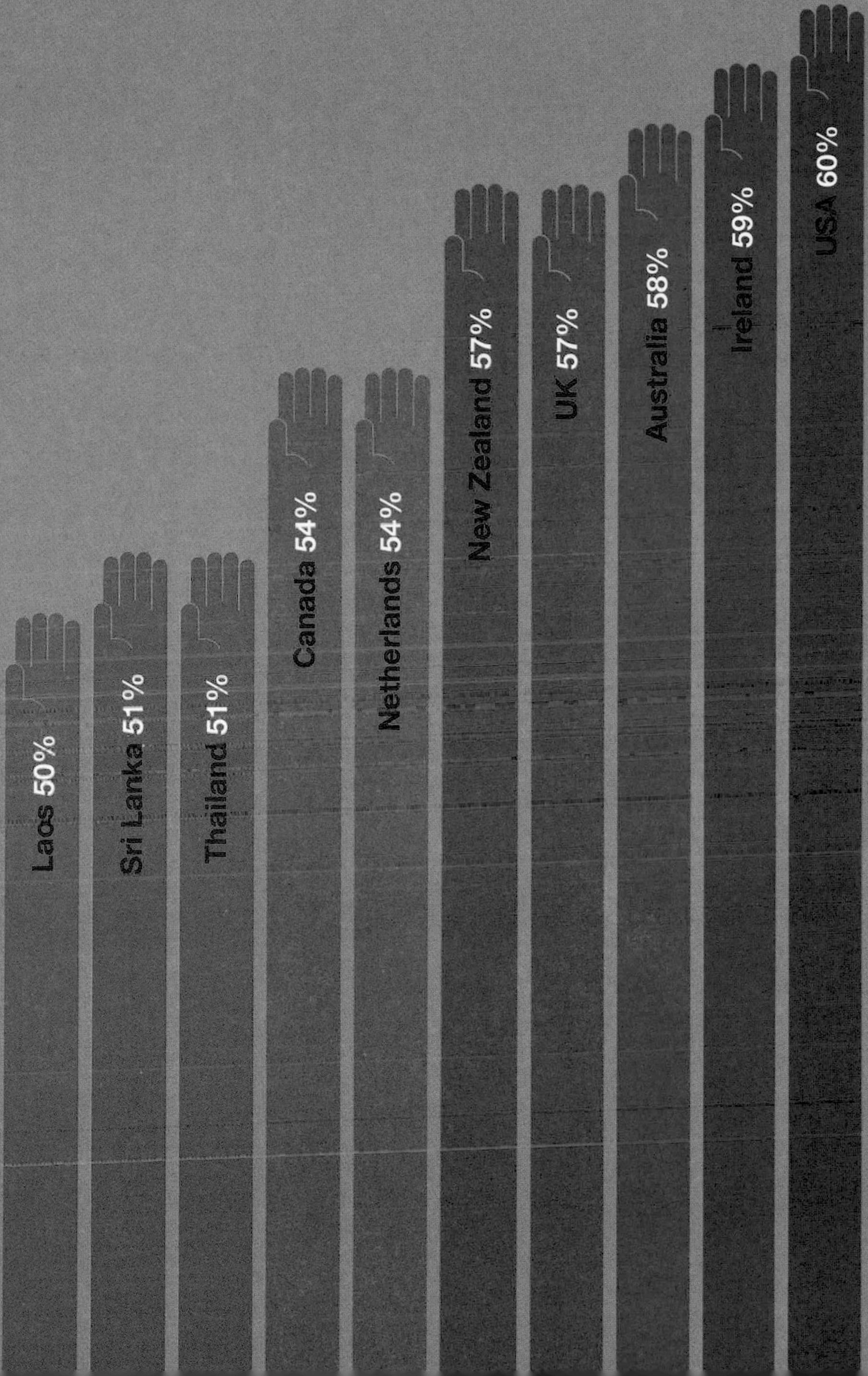

Laos 50%

Sri Lanka 51%

Thailand 51%

Canada 54%

Netherlands 54%

New Zealand 57%

UK 57%

Australia 58%

Ireland 59%

USA 60%

Couch potatoes

Average time spent viewing TV a day in hours and minutes

USA
8:21

Hungary
4:24

Greece
4:24

Poland
4:00

Japan
3:54

Canada
3:48

Turkey
3:48

Spain
3:46

UK
3:45

Germany
3:32

France
3:25

Portugal
3:17

New Zealand **3:17**	Czech Republic **3:10**	Slovakia **3:09**
Denmark **3:09**	South Korea **3:05**	Australia **3:05**
Ireland **3:05**	Netherlands **3:04**	Norway **2:54**
Finland **2:50**	Sweden **2:45**	Austria **2:25**

On board

Percentage of women directors on boards of FTSE 100 companies

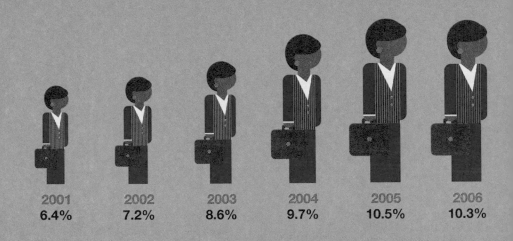

2001	2002	2003	2004	2005	2006
6.4%	7.2%	8.6%	9.7%	10.5%	10.3%

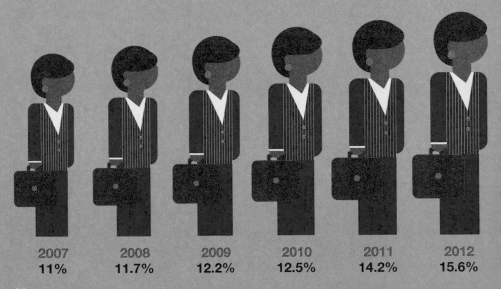

2007	2008	2009	2010	2011	2012
11%	11.7%	12.2%	12.5%	14.2%	15.6%

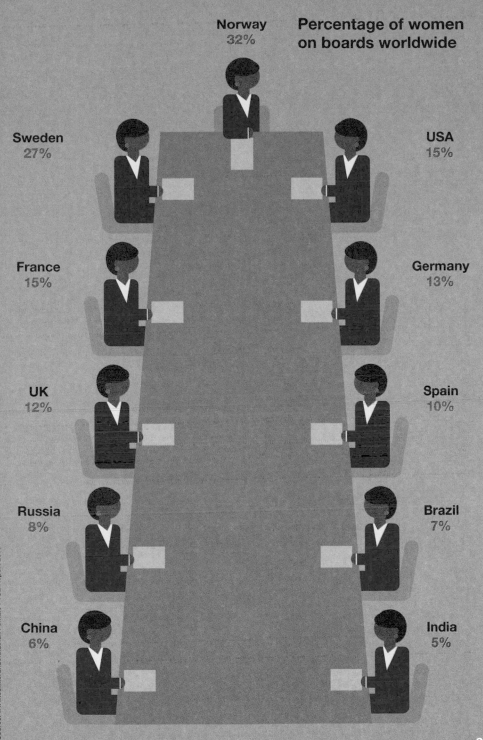

Norway 32%

Percentage of women on boards worldwide

Sweden 27%

USA 15%

France 15%

Germany 13%

UK 12%

Spain 10%

Russia 8%

Brazil 7%

China 6%

India 5%

21

Café culture

Signature drinks created by the recent winners of the World Barista Championships

**2011
Alejandro Mendez
El Salvador**

Espresso with infusion of coffee mucilage (a tea made with dried coffee flowers) and a tea made from cascara (dried coffee cherries)

**2010
Michael Phillips
USA**

3 espressos from 1 terroir: the Coope Dopa Cooperative in Santa María de Dota, Tarrazú, Costa Rica

**2009
Gwilym Davies
UK**

Espresso with an infusion of butter, cinnamon, orange peel, soft brown sugar syrup, and dark chocolate

**2008
Stephen Morrissey
Ireland**

Chocolate and espresso chantilly, milk and cinnamon panna cotta, topped with blueberry jelly and ground freeze-dried blueberries. Solid until the last moment, then blow-torched into a liquid

2007
James Hoffmann
UK

Espresso with biscotti foam,
milk chocolate, and
tobacco-infused cream

2006
Klaus Thomsen
Denmark

Espresso with panna cotta
and coffee foam

2005
Troels Overdal Poulsen
Denmark

Espresso with green
Madagascar pepper, lavender
syrup, and sugar drops

2004
Tim Wendelboe
Norway

Espresso with whisked mascarpone,
eggs, confectioners' sugar, and
marsala syrup, topped with grated
orange-flavored
chocolate

mfbook

A snapshot of the ratio of male to female users in 50 countries with the most Facebook users

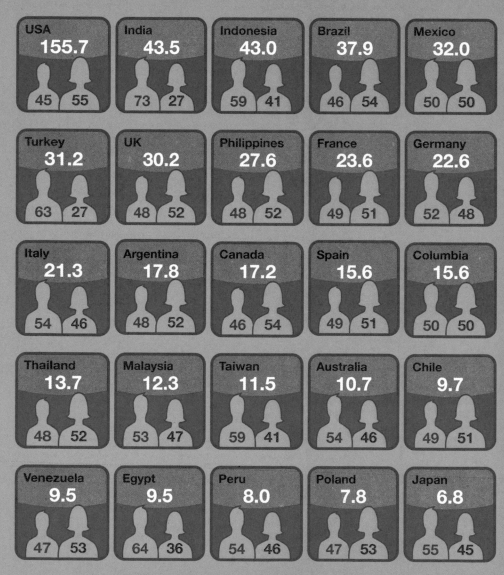

Country	Value	Male	Female
USA	155.7	45	55
India	43.5	73	27
Indonesia	43.0	59	41
Brazil	37.9	46	54
Mexico	32.0	50	50
Turkey	31.2	63	27
UK	30.2	48	52
Philippines	27.6	48	52
France	23.6	49	51
Germany	22.6	52	48
Italy	21.3	54	46
Argentina	17.8	48	52
Canada	17.2	46	54
Spain	15.6	49	51
Columbia	15.6	50	50
Thailand	13.7	48	52
Malaysia	12.3	53	47
Taiwan	11.5	59	41
Australia	10.7	54	46
Chile	9.7	49	51
Venezuela	9.5	47	53
Egypt	9.5	64	36
Peru	8.0	54	46
Poland	7.8	47	53
Japan	6.8	55	45

24

Key

Users (in millions) → Country **1.0**

Ratio of male to female users → 50 | 50

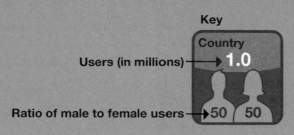

Pakistan	Netherlands	South Korea	Russia	Saudi Arabia
6.1	**6.0**	**5.7**	**5.3**	**4.9**
68 / 32	48 / 52	58 / 42	48 / 52	68 / 32

South Africa	Sweden	Belgium	Romania	Nigeria
4.8	**4.6**	**4.5**	**4.4**	**4.2**
49 / 51	49 / 51	51 / 49	50 / 50	68 / 32

Ecuador	Portugal	Morocco	Hungary	Vietnam
4.2	**4.2**	**4.2**	**3.9**	**3.8**
52 / 48	51 / 49	62 / 38	48 / 52	54 / 46

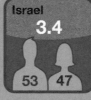

Hong Kong	Greece	Czech Rep.	Israel	Serbia
3.7	**3.6**	**3.6**	**3.4**	**3.3**
48 / 52	56 / 44	49 / 51	53 / 47	55 / 45

Algeria	Tunisia	UAE	Denmark	Switzerland
3.2	**2.9**	**2.8**	**2.8**	**2.8**
68 / 32	58 / 42	67 / 33	49 / 51	52 / 48

I have a dream

A visual representation, known as a word cloud, showing the frequency with which words appear in Martin Luther King's "I Have a Dream" speech. The bigger the word, the more often it is used

Negro
ring
dream
today
come
nation
satisfied
justice
children
able
free
hundred
years
great
American
later
time
long
Georgia
Mississippi
sweltering
injustice
rights
still
last
make
brothers
brotherhood
land
suffering
hope
now
destiny
segregation
sing
stand
mountain
vote
new
believe
live
note
cities
transform
One
former
sons
allow
meaning
mighty
Negro's
brutality
made
little
thee
realize
rise
valley
funds
redemptive
insufficient
something
true
right
bright
heat
jail
places
even
hill
satisfy
physical
gain
despair
walk
concerned
created
slaves
promises
left
rightful
dripping
owners
yes
ocean
scarred

Spam, spam, spam

The rise and fall of spam mail. The huge reduction in the volume of spam mail in 2011 was the result of Operation b107—a Microsoft-led attack on the Rustock botnet, one of the major spam generators

 Total emails sent per day (billions)

 Total spam emails sent per day (billions)

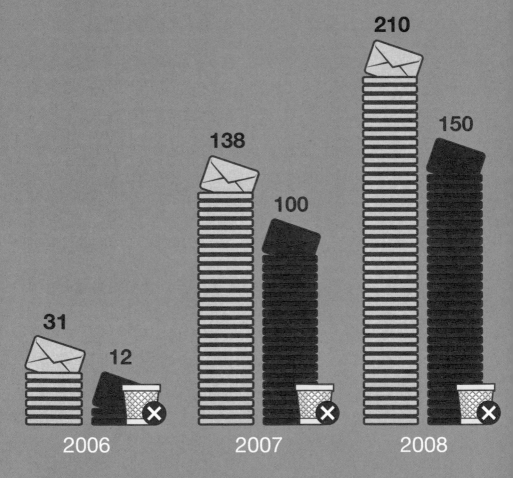

31 12 2006

138 100 2007

210 150 2008

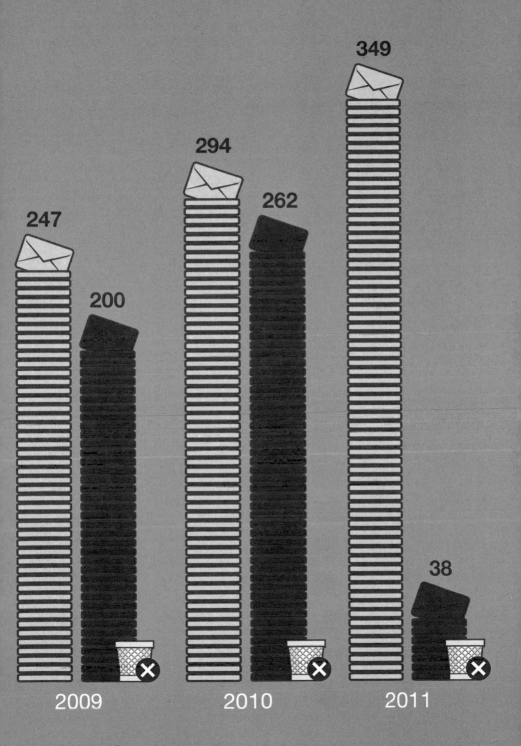

247 200 2009

294 262 2010

349 38 2011

Going viral

Videos with the most hits on YouTube, excluding professional music and ads

An Experiment
225.6m

**Evolution
of Dance**
191.9m

**Video Stroboscopy
of the Vocal Cords**
152.2m

**Best Ever!!!
(sex blog)**
149m

**Jeff Dunham:
Achmed the
Dead Terrorist**
148.5m

**The Sneezing
Baby Panda**
132.3m

**The Potter
Puppet Pals**
122.7m

Charlie bit my finger—again!
429.7m

Bodybuilder Tamer El Shahat flexes biceps
112.2m

BallsCrash
121m

Flower power

Some facts about the internationally renowned Chelsea Flower Show, which takes place annually in London, UK

The Great Pavilion is 129,000 sq ft (12,000m²)—the same size as 2 soccer pitches, an area large enough to park 500 London buses

The urban spaces are 16ft x 13ft (7m x 5m) and courtyard gardens are 16ft x 13ft (5m x 4m)

It takes 800 people just over 3 weeks to build the show, but only 5 days to clear the grounds

The planning of each show takes 15 months

Over 98% of materials used at Chelsea, including glass, plastic, and paper, are recycled

Nearly 600 new plants have been launched at the show

157,000 visitors attend Chelsea each year—the number has been capped since 1988

A 328ft-deep borehole was drilled in 2006 to source water for irrigating gardens and floral exhibits

A show garden can range in size from 33ft x 33ft (10m x 10m) to 33ft x 72ft (10m x 22m)

It takes up to 3 weeks to build a show garden, 10 days to build a courtyard and an urban garden

The show has been held at the Royal Hospital since 1913

On average 76,000 paper and 89,000 recycled plastic cups are used

Around, 2,000 bottles of champagne and 46,500 glasses of Pimms are drunk, 65,000 cups of Fairtrade tea and coffee are served, and 18,000 sandwiches are consumed

There are 600 exhibitors from all over the world, 15 show gardens, 21 small gardens, over 100 floral exhibitors, more than 60 floristry and floral arrangement displays, and over 250 garden product exhibitors

The showground covers 11 acres (4.5ha)

World Cup winners

The top scorers and assist-makers in FIFA Soccer
World Cup tournaments since 1966

1966 England

Eusébio
(POR)
9 goals

Siegfried
Held
(GER)
4 assists

Uwe
Seeler
(GER)
4 assists

1970 Mexico

Gerd
Müller
(GER)
10 goals

Pelé
(BRA)
5 assists

1974 West Germany

Grzegorz
Lato
(POL)
7 goals

Robert
Gadocha
(POL)
5 assists

1978 Argentina

Mario
Kempes
(ARG)
6 goals

René van de
Kerkhof
(NED)
3 assists

1982 Spain

Paolo
Rossi
(ITA)
6 goals

Pierre
Littbarski
(GER)
5 assists

1986 Mexico

Gary
Lineker
(ENG)
6 goals

Diego
Maradona
(ARG)
5 assists

1990 Italy

Salvatore
Schillaci
(ITA)
6 goals

Andreas
Brehme
(GER)
3 assists

1994 USA

Hristo
Stoitchkov
(BUL)
6 goals

Oleg
Salenko
(RUS)
6 goals

Thomas
Hässler
(GER)
5 assists

1998 France

Davor
Šuker
(CRO)
6 goals

Juan
Verón
(ARG)
3 assists

2002 S. Korea/Japan

Ronaldo
(BRA)
8 goals

Michael
Ballack
(GER)
4 assists

2006 Germany

Miroslav
Klose
(GER)
5 goals

Francesco
Totti
(ITA)
4 assists

2010 South Africa

Thomas
Müller
(GER)
5 goals
3 assists

David
Villa
(SPA)
5 goals

Wesley
Sneijder
(NED)
5 goals

Diego
Forlán
(URU)
5 goals

Kaká
(BRA)
3 assists

Mesut
Özil
(GER)
3 assists

Bastian
Schweinsteiger
(GER)
3 assists

Dirk
Kuijt
(NED)
3 assists

A world of debt

Public debt as a percentage of GDP by country

Japan 225.8%	Saint Kitts & Nevis 185.0%	Lebanon 150.7%	Zimbabwe 149.0%	Greece 144.0%
Ireland 94.2%	France 83.5%	Portugal 83.2%	Egypt 80.5%	Hungary 79.6%
Spain 63.4%	Brazil 60.8%	WORLD 59.3%	Albania 59.3%	Bahrain 59.2%
Argentina 50.3%	Pakistan 49.9%	Turkey 48.1%	Norway 47.7%	Denmark 46.6%
Canada 34.0%	Syria 29.8%	Indonesia 26.4%	New Zealand 25.5%	Australia 22.4%

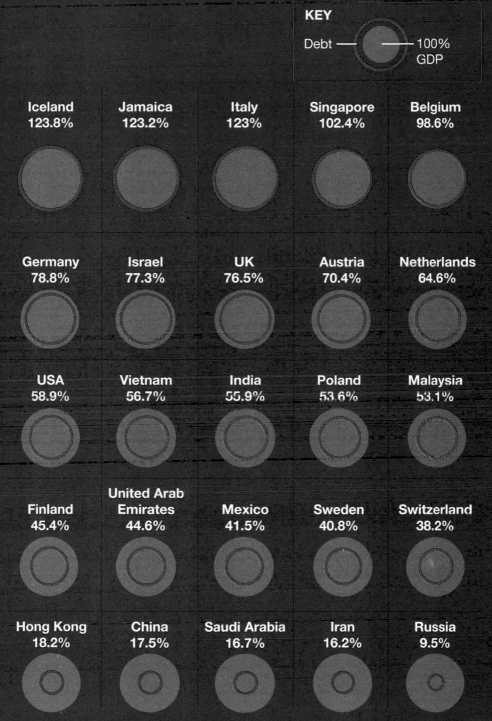

KEY

Debt —— ——100% GDP

| Iceland 123.8% | Jamaica 123.2% | Italy 123% | Singapore 102.4% | Belgium 98.6% |

| Germany 78.8% | Israel 77.3% | UK 76.5% | Austria 70.4% | Netherlands 64.6% |

| USA 58.9% | Vietnam 56.7% | India 55.9% | Poland 53.6% | Malaysia 53.1% |

| Finland 45.4% | United Arab Emirates 44.6% | Mexico 41.5% | Sweden 40.8% | Switzerland 38.2% |

| Hong Kong 18.2% | China 17.5% | Saudi Arabia 16.7% | Iran 16.2% | Russia 9.5% |

Fish nets

Annual global catch of commercial fish species, measured in tons

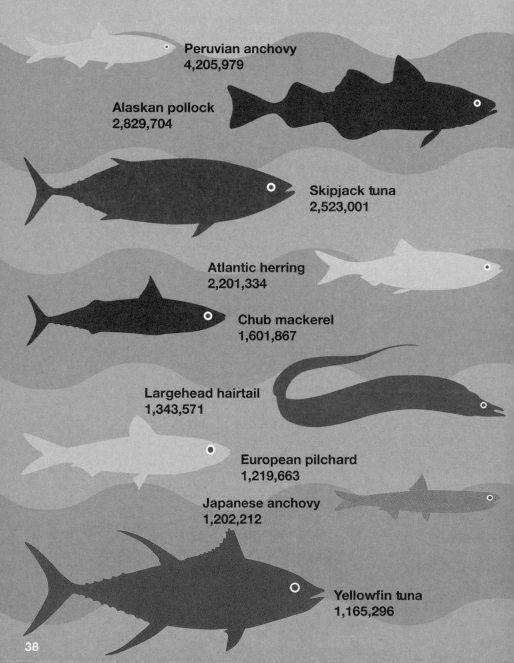

Peruvian anchovy
4,205,979

Alaskan pollock
2,829,704

Skipjack tuna
2,523,001

Atlantic herring
2,201,334

Chub mackerel
1,601,867

Largehead hairtail
1,343,571

European pilchard
1,219,663

Japanese anchovy
1,202,212

Yellowfin tuna
1,165,296

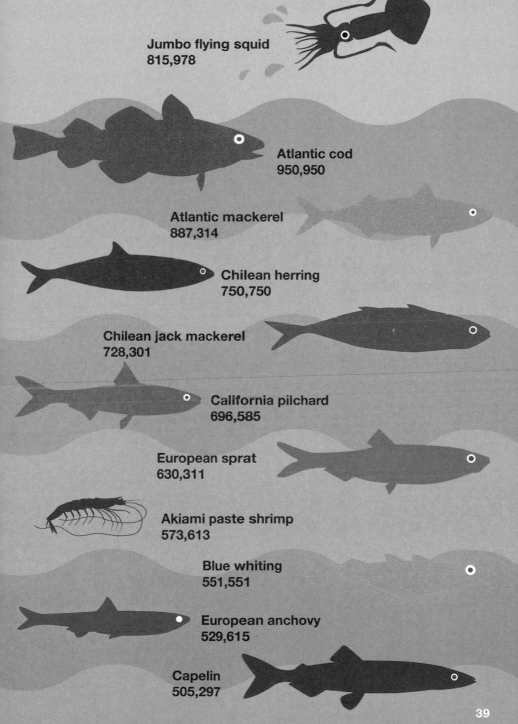

Jumbo flying squid
815,978

Atlantic cod
950,950

Atlantic mackerel
887,314

Chilean herring
750,750

Chilean jack mackerel
728,301

California pilchard
696,585

European sprat
630,311

Akiami paste shrimp
573,613

Blue whiting
551,551

European anchovy
529,615

Capelin
505,297

Crowded capitals

The most densely populated capital cities in the world

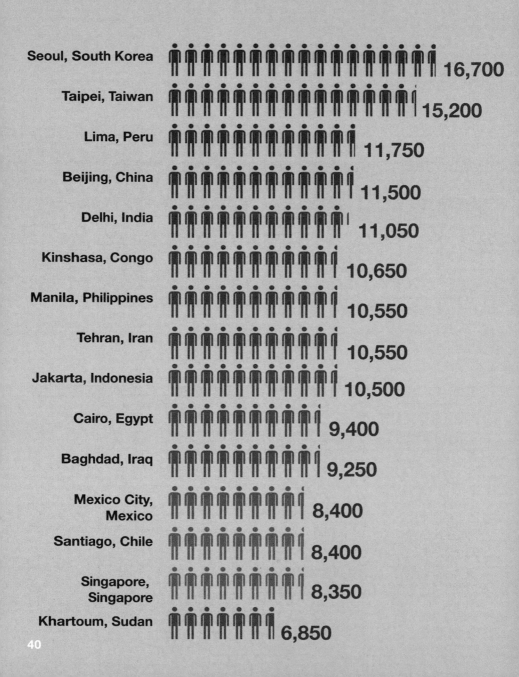

Seoul, South Korea — 16,700

Taipei, Taiwan — 15,200

Lima, Peru — 11,750

Beijing, China — 11,500

Delhi, India — 11,050

Kinshasa, Congo — 10,650

Manila, Philippines — 10,550

Tehran, Iran — 10,550

Jakarta, Indonesia — 10,500

Cairo, Egypt — 9,400

Baghdad, Iraq — 9,250

Mexico City, Mexico — 8,400

Santiago, Chile — 8,400

Singapore, Singapore — 8,350

Khartoum, Sudan — 6,850

= 1,000 people per km²

City	Density
Bangkok, Thailand	6,450
Athens, Greece	5,400
Ankara, Turkey	5,300
Madrid, Spain	5,200
London, UK	5,100
Tel Aviv, Israel	5,050
Buenos Aires, Argentina	4,950
Moscow, Russia	4,900
Tokyo, Japan	4,750
Warsaw, Poland	4,300
Tashkent, Uzbekistan	4,150
Baku, Azerbaijan	3,850
Berlin, Germany	3,750
Riyadh, Saudi Arabia	3,650
Paris, France	3,550

Car 007

Iconic cars driven by 007 in the James Bond movies

Dr No (1962)
Sunbeam Alpine

From Russia With Love (1963)
Bentley

Goldfinger (1964)
Aston Martin DB5

Thunderball (1965)
Aston Martin DBS

On Her Majesty's Secret Service (1969)
Aston Martin DBS

The Spy Who Loved Me (1977)
Lotus Esprit S1
(Car/Sub)

For Your Eyes Only (1981)
Lotus Esprit Turbo

The Living Daylights (1987)
Aston Martin V8 Vantage

GoldenEye (1996)
BMW Z3

Tomorrow Never Dies (1997)
BMW 750iL

The World Is Not Enough (1999)
BMW Z8

Die Another Day (2002)
Aston Martin V12 vanquish

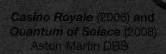

Casino Royale (2006) and
Quantum of Solace (2008)
Aston Martin DBS

43

Lost in translation

How noises are written in different languages

Parp!	**Waah!**	**Tweet**
Pups!	**Wäh-wäh!**	**Piep**
Bu!	**Ogyaa!**	**Pii pii**
Pook!	**Ua-ua!**	**Fiyt-fiyt**
Pedo!	Buá buá!	Pio pio
Prout!	Ouin ouin!	Cui cui

Mwah	**Woof!**	**Toot toot**
Schmatz	**Wau wau!**	**Tut**
Chū	**Wan wan!**	**Pū pū**
Chmoc	**Gav gav!**	**Bi-bi**
Muac	Guau guau!	Pip pip
Smack	**Ouah ouah!**	**Tut-tut**

■ English
■ German
■ Japanese
■ Russian
□ Spanish
■ French

Yum yum
Mampf mampf
Mogu mogu
Njam-njam
Ñam ñam
Miam miam

Ring ring
Klingeling
Jiririri
Dzyn'-dzyn'
Rin rin
Dring dring

Gulp
Schluck
Goku
Glyg
Glup
Glouglou

Achoo!
Hatschi!
Hakushon!
Apchkhi!
Achú!
Atchoum!

Nee naw!
Tatütata!
Pīpō pīpō!
Wiu-wiu!
Nino-nino!
Pin pon!

Drip drip
Platsch
Pota pota
Kap kap
Pluip pluip
Plic plic

45

Lucky dip

The largest lottery jackpot records worldwide by country (approximate USD)

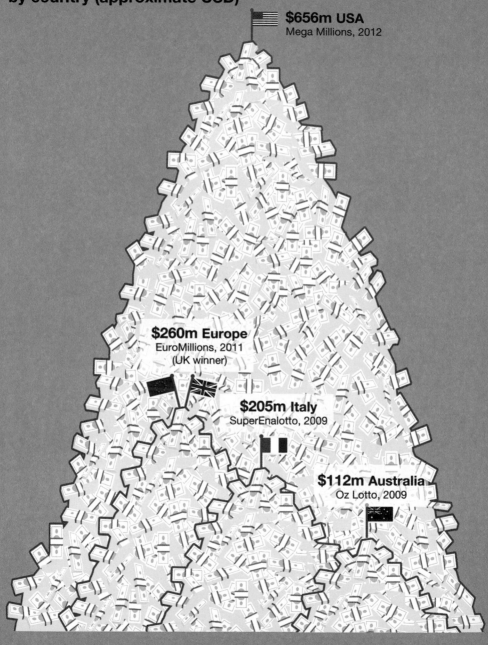

$656m USA
Mega Millions, 2012

$260m Europe
EuroMillions, 2011
(UK winner)

$205m Italy
SuperEnalotto, 2009

$112m Australia
Oz Lotto, 2009

Most common EuroMillions winning numbers

3   4   5   12   19   38   50

$67m
Germany
Lotto 6aus49,
2007

$65m
UK
Lotto,
1996

$46m
Brazil
Mega-Sena,
2010

$31m
France
Super Loto,
2006

$30m
Ireland
Lotto,
2008

$17m
Philippines
Grand Lotto
6/55, 2010

$15m
Belgium
Loterie
Nationale/
Nationale
Loterij,
2008

47

Winds of change

Wind power capacity (in megawatts) of countries around the world

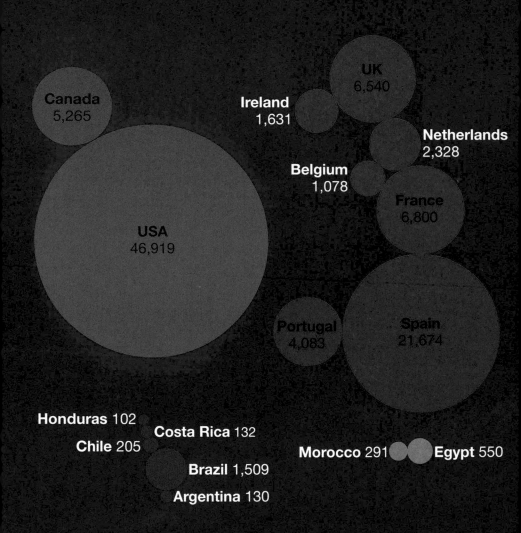

Canada 5,265

Ireland 1,631

UK 6,540

Netherlands 2,328

Belgium 1,078

France 6,800

USA 46,919

Portugal 4,083

Spain 21,674

Honduras 102

Costa Rica 132

Chile 205

Brazil 1,509

Argentina 130

Morocco 291

Egypt 550

- Africa & Middle East
- Asia
- Europe
- Latin America & Caribbean
- North America
- Pacific Region

Sweden 2,970

Denmark 3,871

Poland 1,616

Germany 29,060

China 62,364

Austria 1,084

Italy 6,737

Greece 1,629

Turkey 1,799

India 16,084

South Korea 407

Taiwan 564

Japan 2,501

Australia 2,224

New Zealand 623

49

The cost of canvas

The world's most expensive paintings sold at auction, ranked by inflation-adjusted value (USD)

1 $254,000,000

The Card Players
Paul Cezanne,1892/93

Seller: George Embiricos
Buyer: Royal family of Qatar

2 $159,400,000

No. 5, 1948
Jackson Pollock,1948

Seller: David Geffen
Buyer: Unknown

3 $156,500,000

Woman III
Willem de Kooning,1953

Seller: David Geffen
Buyer: Steven A. Cohen

7 $126,400,000

Garçon à la pipe
Pablo Picasso,1905

Seller: Greentree Foundation
Buyer: Barilla Group

8 $119,900,000

The Scream
Edvard Munch, 1892

Seller: Petter Olsen
Buyer: Anonymous

9 $112,000,000

Nude, Green Leaves and Bust
Pablo Picasso,1932

Seller: Frances Lasker Brody estate
Buyer: Unknown

4

$152,600,000

Portrait of Adele Bloch-Bauer I
Gustav Klimt,1907
Seller: Maria Altmann
Buyer: Ronald Lauder

5

$146,500,000

Portrait of Dr Gachet
Vincent van Gogh,1890
Seller: Siegfried Kramarsky family
Buyer: Ryoei Saito

6

$138,700,000

Bal du moulin de la Galette
Pierre-Auguste Renoir,1876
Seller: Betsey Whitney
Buyer: Ryoei Saito

10

$108,000,000

Portrait of Joseph Roulin
Vincent van Gogh,1889
Seller: Private collection
Buyer: MOMA, New York

11

$107,900,000

Dora Maar au Chat
Pablo Picasso,1941
Seller: Gidwitz family
Buyer: Boris Ivanishvili

12

$107,200,000

Irises
Vincent van Gogh,1889
Seller: Joan Whitney Payson
Buyer: Alan Bond

Lexicographer's dream

Some of the longest words in different languages
and what they mean

Kraftfahrzeug–Haftpflichtversicherung

German: motor vehicle liability insurance

anticonstitutionnellement

French: something against the constitution

lentokonesuihkuturbiinimoottoriapumekaanikkoaliupseerioppilas

Finnish: technical warrant officer trainee specialized in aircraft jet engines

pneumonoultramicroscopicsilicovolcanokoniosis

English: a lung disease

electroencefalografistas

Spanish: electroencephalograph technicians

NAGSISIPAGSISINUNGASINUNGALINGAN

Tagalog: trying to tell lies

kindercarnavalsoptochtvoorbereidingswerkzaamheden

Dutch: preparation activities for a children's carnival procession

uusaastaöövastuvõtuhommikuidüll

Estonian: an ideal morning after the New Year

REALISATIONSVINSTBESKATTNING

Swedish: capital gains tax

Megszentségtelenithetetlenségeskedéseitekért

Hungarian: the impossibility of committing multiple acts of desecration

частнопредпринимательскими

Russian: something owned by an entrepreneur

Hemline index

In 1926 an economic theory was proposed that the fashionable length of women's skirts in any year reflected the global economic circumstances: the shorter the skirt the better the conditions. This theory has been put to the test many times. Most recently researchers in the Netherlands suggested there is a correlation but that there is also a three-year time lag between the onset of economic woes and the lengthening of skirt hemlines

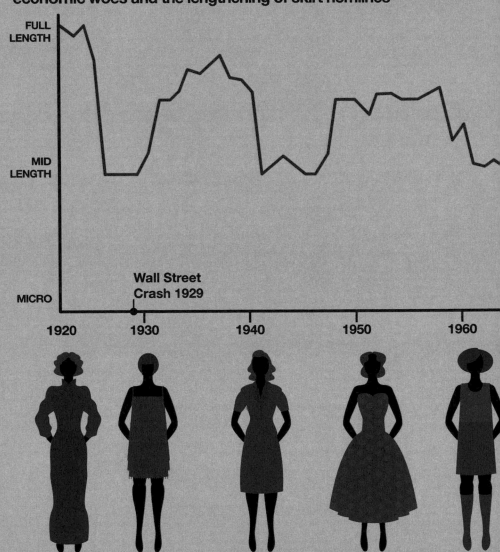

FULL LENGTH

MID LENGTH

MICRO

Wall Street Crash 1929

1920　1930　1940　1950　1960

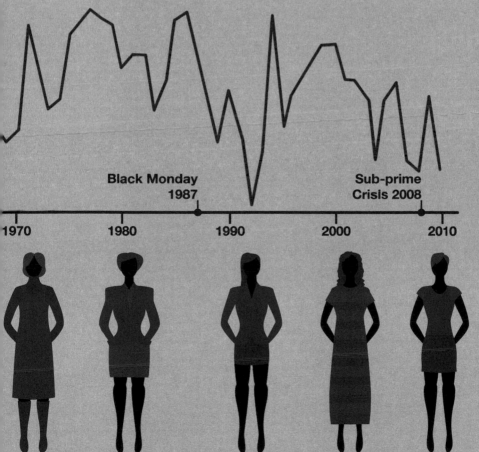

Black Monday
1987

Sub-prime
Crisis 2008

1970   1980   1990   2000   2010

Backhanders

The extent of perceived corruption in
the public sectors of 183 countries

Somalia North Korea
Turkmenistan Sudan
Equatorial Guinea Burundi
Angola Kyrgyzstan Guinea
Papua New Guinea Nepal Laos
Congo Republic Central African Republic
Timor-Leste Russia Nigeria Mauritania
Niger Nicaragua Maldives Lebanon Guyana
Dominican Republic Armenia Solomon Islands
Ethiopia Ecuador Bangladesh Bolivia Vietnam Senegal
São Tomé & Príncipe Mexico Malawi Madagascar Indonesia
Kiribati India Zambia Trinidad & Tobago Liberia Bosnia & Herzegovina
Greece El Salvador Colombia Vanuatu Lesotho Gambia Romania
South Africa Georgia Turkey Latvia Cuba Malaysia Saudi Arabia Namibia
Rwanda Mauritius Bahrain Dominica Brunei South Korea Poland Cape Verde
Botswana Spain Cyprus Estonia United Arab Emirates Uruguay St Lucia France
Germany Iceland Hong Kong Luxembourg Canada Switzerland Australia Netherlands Norway

Larger type indicates higher level
of perceived corruption

Afghanistan Uzbekistan
Iraq Haiti Venezuela
Libya D.R. Congo Chad
Cambodia Zimbabwe Paraguay
Kenya Guinea-Bissau Côte d'Ivoire
Ukraine Tajikistan Uganda Togo
Comoros Belarus Sierra Leone Pakistan
Eritrea Cameroon Syria Philippines Honduras
Mozambique Mongolia Kazakhstan Iran Guatemala
Moldova Kosovo Egypt Algeria Tanzania Suriname
Gabon Dijbouti Burkina Faso Benin Argentina Tonga Swaziland
Sri Lanka Serbia Panama Jamaica Bulgaria Thailand Peru Morocco
China Tunisia Brazil Samoa Italy Ghana Slovakia Montenegro Croatia
Czech Republic Jordan Kuwait Hungary Seychelles Oman Lithuania Costa Rica
Puerto Rico Malta Bhutan St Vincent & the Grenadines Israel Slovenia Taiwan Portugal
United States Qatar Chile Bahamas Ireland Belgium UK Barbados Austria Japan
Singapore Sweden Finland Denmark New Zealand

Cash cows

The price (USD) and the date of sale of some of the most expensive artworks by British artist Damien Hirst

The Golden Calf
$19,027,496
September 15 2008

Lullaby Spring
$17,752,437
June 21 2007

The Kingdom
$17,585,525
September 15 2008

Memories of / Moments with You
$4,813,775
September 15 2008

The Dream
$4,298,786
September 16 2008

Ascended
$4,195,788
September 16 2008

After the Flood
$3,268,806
September 15 2008

Amphotericin B, 1993
$3,177,000
May 15 2008

The Triumvirate
$3,165,808
September 15 2008

D, A, B, D, A.
$2,650,818
September 15 2008

Bromphenol Red
$2,640,000
February 14 2008

Adam and Eve
$2,617,000
November 14 2007

All You Need Is Love
$2,420,000
February 14 2008

Notechis Ater Humphreysi (no. 0072)
$2,392,000
May 16 2007

The Rose Window, Durham Cathedral
$2,341,824
September 15 2008

Fragments of Paradise
$9,551,682
September 15 2008

**Here Today,
Gone Tomorrow**
$5,431,763
September 15 2008

**The Black Sheep with
the Golden Horn**
$4,813,775
September 15 2008

**Away from the
Flock, Divided**
$3,376,000
May 5 2006

Love You
$3,300,000
February 14 2008

The Abyss
$3,268,806
September 15 2008

Reincarnated
$2,959,812
September 16 2008

**The Importance of Elsewhere
—The Kingdom of Heaven**
$2,959,812
June 29 2008

**Apolopoprotein
A-1**
$2,841,000
November 14 2007

End of the Line
$2,547,820
September 15 2008

Afterlife
$2,547,820
September 15 2008

Rapture
$2,547,820
July 1 2008

Love Affair, 2001
$2,281,000
November 15 2007

**Beautiful Explosion
of Vanity Painting ...**
$2,096,744
June 21 2007

Twenty-Nine Pills
$2,032,830
September 15 2008

59

Extinct

Some species declared extinct since 1945, their native area, and the date of their extinction

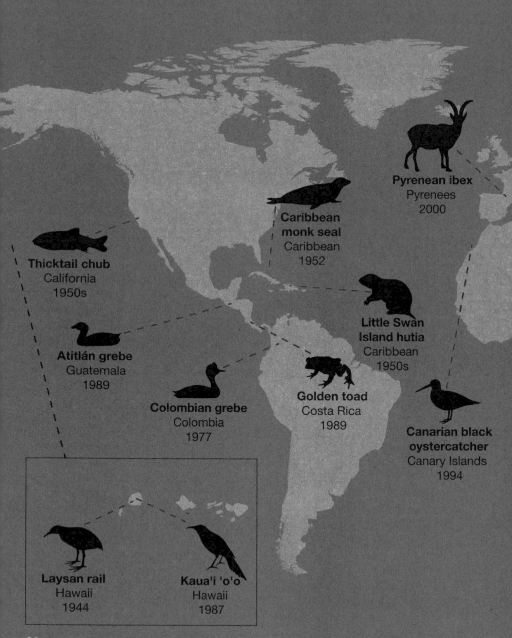

Pyrenean ibex
Pyrenees
2000

Caribbean monk seal
Caribbean
1952

Thicktail chub
California
1950s

Little Swan Island hutia
Caribbean
1950s

Atitlán grebe
Guatemala
1989

Colombian grebe
Colombia
1977

Golden toad
Costa Rica
1989

Canarian black oystercatcher
Canary Islands
1994

Laysan rail
Hawaii
1944

Kaua'i 'o'o
Hawaii
1987

Santo Stefano lizard
Santo Stefano Island
1965

Palestinian painted frog
Israel
1955

Caspian tiger
Western and Central Asia
1950

Japanese sea lion
Japan and Korea
1974

Arabian ostrich
Jordan
1966

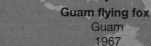

Javan tiger
Indonesia
1972

Wake Island rail
Wake Atoll
1945

Western black rhinoceros
Central Africa
2006

Guam flying fox
Guam
1967

Round Island burrowing boa
Mauritius
1975

Bushwren
New Zealand
1972

Crescent nail-tail wallaby
Australia
1950s

South Island piopio
New Zealand
1963

Facial topiary

Terms specified by the American Mustache Institute to describe some common mustache styles

Chevron

Dalí

English

Fu Manchu

Handlebar

Horseshoe

Imperial

Lampshade

Painter's brush

62

Petit handlebar · Toothbrush · Walrus

········· Pencil mustaches ·········

········· Pyramidal mustaches ·········

Come fly with me

The world's busiest airports ranked by numbers of passengers arriving and departing annually

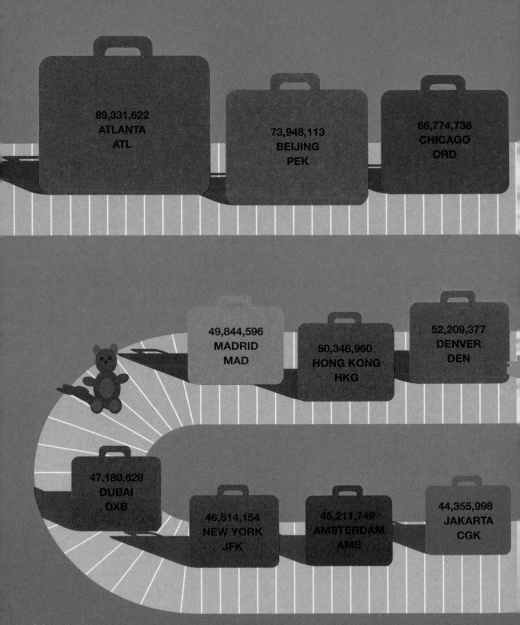

89,331,622
ATLANTA
ATL

73,948,113
BEIJING
PEK

66,774,738
CHICAGO
ORD

49,844,596
MADRID
MAD

50,348,960
HONG KONG
HKG

52,209,377
DENVER
DEN

47,180,628
DUBAI
DXB

46,514,154
NEW YORK
JFK

45,211,749
AMSTERDAM
AMS

44,355,998
JAKARTA
CGK

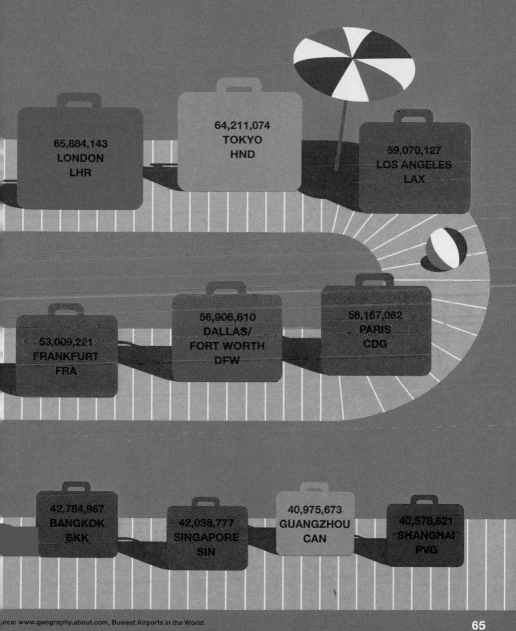

65,884,143
LONDON
LHR

64,211,074
TOKYO
HND

59,070,127
LOS ANGELES
LAX

53,009,221
FRANKFURT
FRA

56,906,610
DALLAS/
FORT WORTH
DFW

58,167,062
PARIS
CDG

42,784,967
BANGKOK
BKK

42,038,777
SINGAPORE
SIN

40,975,673
GUANGZHOU
CAN

40,578,621
SHANGHAI
PVG

urce: www.geography.about.com, Busiest Airports in the World

Not-So-Angry Birds

The most successful paid-for app of all time has generated some astonishing statistics since its launch in December 2009

Players have played collectively 200,000 years in total

The total playing time per day was 300 million minutes

500 million downloads in 2 years

Angry Birds Space launched in March 2012 with a video announcement from the International Space Station

Players have flung 400 billion birds

Players have collected 44 billion stars

Players have already gone through 266 billion levels

Jaws

The relative bite strength of different animals

Human

Mastiff

1

4.4

African lion

Mountain gorilla

10.3

10.8

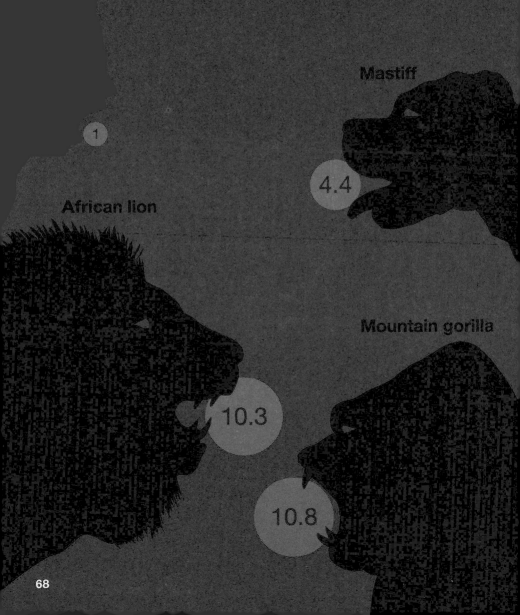

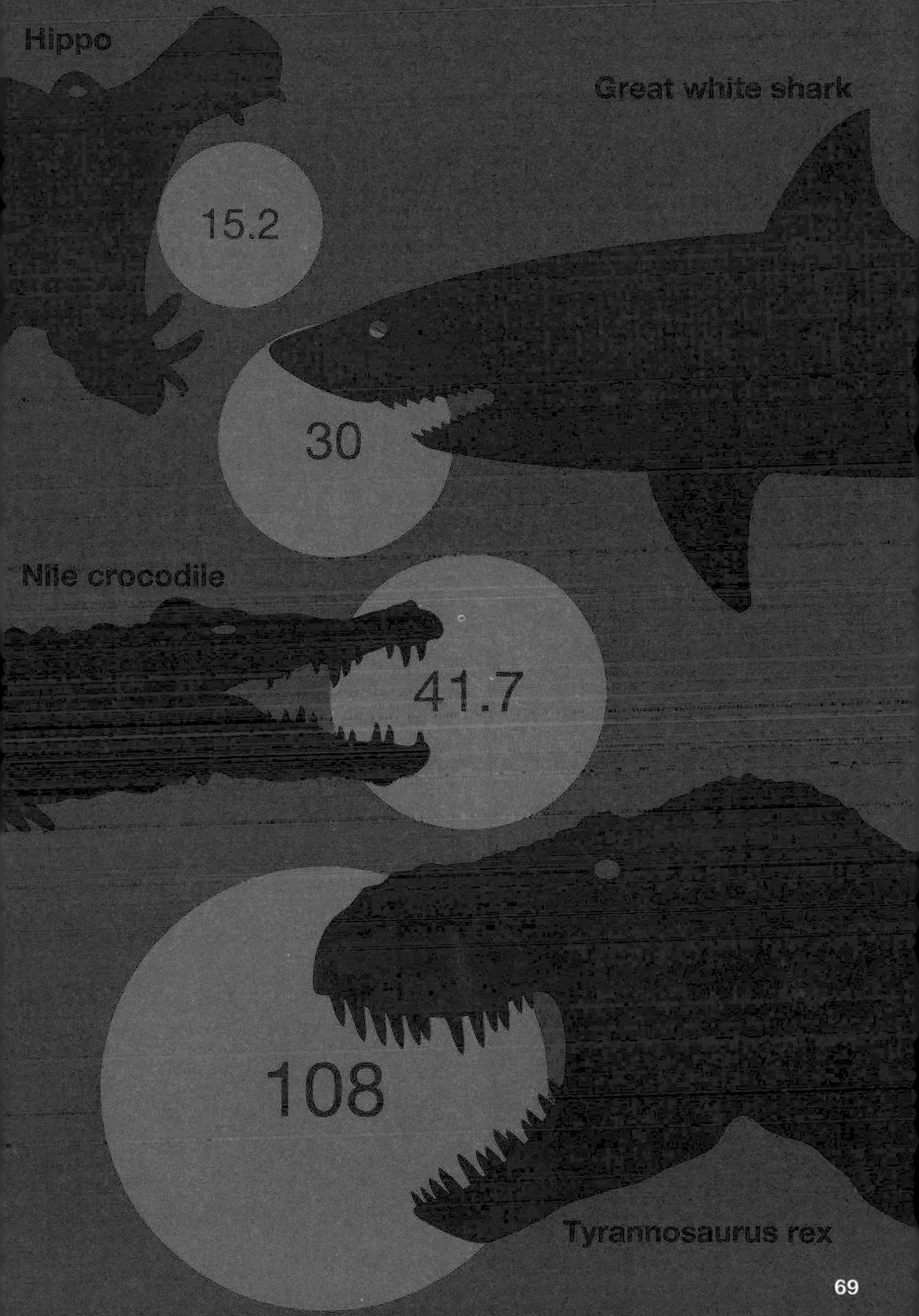

Hippo

Great white shark

15.2

30

Nile crocodile

41.7

108

Tyrannosaurus rex

Diplomatic parking

Average annual number of unpaid parking violations per diplomat in New York City

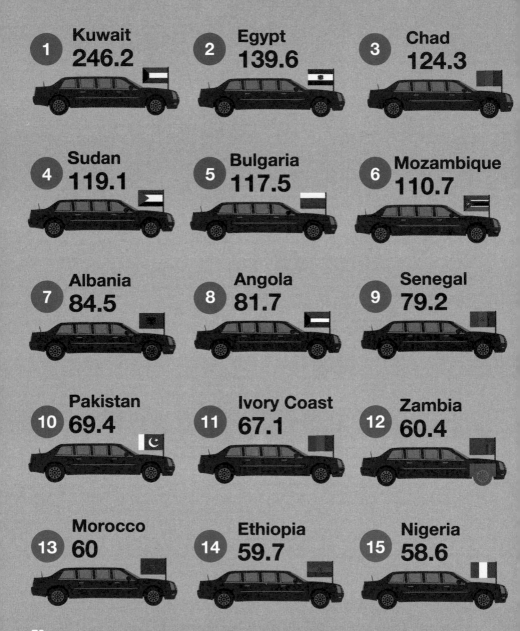

1 Kuwait 246.2

2 Egypt 139.6

3 Chad 124.3

4 Sudan 119.1

5 Bulgaria 117.5

6 Mozambique 110.7

7 Albania 84.5

8 Angola 81.7

9 Senegal 79.2

10 Pakistan 69.4

11 Ivory Coast 67.1

12 Zambia 60.4

13 Morocco 60

14 Ethiopia 59.7

15 Nigeria 58.6

70

16 Syria 52.7

17 Benin 49.8

18 Zimbabwe 45.6

19 Cameroon 43.6

20 Serbia & Montenegro 38

21 Burundi 37.7

22 Bahrain 37.7

23 Mali 37.4

24 Indonesia 36.1

25 Guinea 34.8

26 South Africa 34

27 Saudi Arabia 33.8

28 Bangladesh 33

29 Brazil 29.9

30 Sierra Leone 25.6

31 Algeria 25.2

32 Thailand 24.5

33 Kazakhstan 21.1

Oscar time

Length of movies that have won the "Best Picture" award since the start of the Oscars

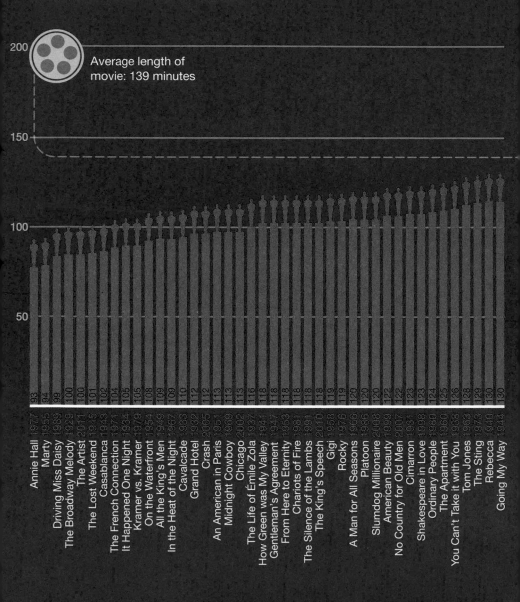

Average length of movie: 139 minutes

Title	Year	Minutes
Annie Hall	1977	93
Marty	1955	94
Driving Miss Daisy	1989	99
The Broadway Melody	1929	100
The Artist	2011	100
The Lost Weekend	1945	101
Casablanca	1943	102
The French Connection	1971	104
It Happened One Night	1934	105
Kramer vs. Kramer	1979	105
On the Waterfront	1954	108
All the King's Men	1949	109
In the Heat of the Night	1967	109
Cavalcade	1933	110
Grand Hotel	1932	112
Crash	2005	112
An American in Paris	1951	113
Midnight Cowboy	1969	113
Chicago	2002	113
The Life of Émile Zola	1937	116
How Green was My Valley	1941	118
Gentleman's Agreement	1947	118
From Here to Eternity	1953	118
Chariots of Fire	1981	118
The Silence of the Lambs	1991	118
The King's Speech	2010	118
Gigi	1958	119
Rocky	1976	119
A Man for All Seasons	1966	120
Platoon	1986	120
Slumdog Millionaire	2008	120
American Beauty	1999	122
No Country for Old Men	2007	122
Cimarron	1931	123
Shakespeare in Love	1998	123
Ordinary People	1980	124
The Apartment	1960	125
You Can't Take it with You	1938	126
Tom Jones	1963	128
The Sting	1973	129
Rebecca	1940	130
Going My Way	1944	130

Length of movie ———
(minutes)

Movie	Year	Length
Terms of Endearment	1983	131
Unforgiven	1992	131
The Hurt Locker	2009	131
Mutiny on the Bounty	1935	132
Million Dollar Baby	2004	132
One Flew Over the Cuckoo's Nest	1975	133
Rain Man	1988	133
Mrs Miniver	1942	134
A Beautiful Mind	2001	135
All About Eve	1950	138
Wings	1928	139
Forrest Gump	1994	141
All Quiet on the Western Front	1930	145
The Departed	2006	151
The Greatest Show on Earth	1952	152
West Side Story	1961	152
Oliver!	1968	153
Hamlet	1948	155
The English Patient	1996	155
Gladiator	2000	155
The Last Emperor	1987	160
The Bridge on the River Kwai	1957	161
Amadeus	1984	161
Out of Africa	1985	161
My Fair Lady	1964	170
Patton	1970	170
The Best Years of Our Lives	1946	172
The Sound of Music	1965	174
The Godfather	1972	175
Braveheart	1995	177
Dances with Wolves	1990	181
Around the World in 80 Days	1956	183
The Deer Hunter	1978	183
The Great Ziegfeld	1936	185
Gandhi	1982	191
Titanic	1997	194
Schindler's List	1993	195
The Godfather Part II	1974	200
The Lord of the Rings: The Return of...	2003	200
Ben-Hur	1959	212
Lawrence of Arabia	1962	216
Gone with the Wind	1939	224

73

Wild rides

The world's fastest roller-coasters

1 **149.1** mph (239.7kph)
Formula Rossa
Ferrari World

Abu Dhabi,
United Arab Emirates

2 **128** mph (205.9kph)
Kingda Ka
Six Flags Great
Adventure

New Jersey, USA

99.4 mph (159.9kph)
Ring Racer
Nürburgring

Rhineland-Palatinate,
Germany

3 **120** mph (193.1kph)
Top Thrill Dragster
Cedar Point

Ohio, USA

6

106.9 mph (172kph)
Dodonpa
Fuji-Q Highland

Yamanashi, Japan

4

5 **100** mph (160.9kph)
**Superman: Escape
from Krypton**
Six Flags Magic
Mountain

California, USA

Tower of Terror II
Dreamworld

Queensland, Australia

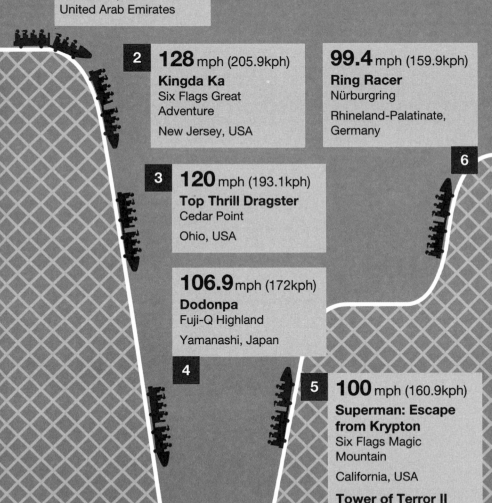

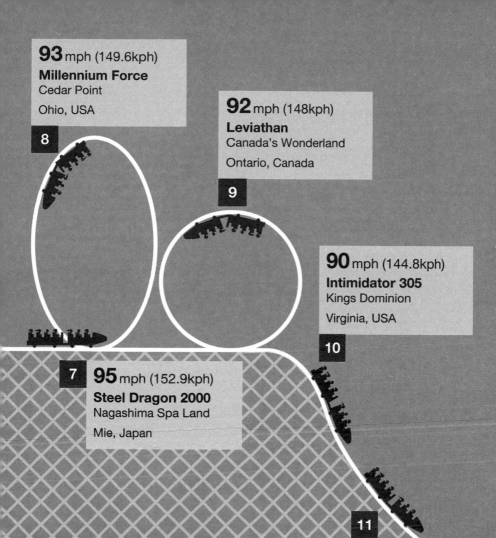

93 mph (149.6kph)
Millennium Force
Cedar Point
Ohio, USA

8

92 mph (148kph)
Leviathan
Canada's Wonderland
Ontario, Canada

9

90 mph (144.8kph)
Intimidator 305
Kings Dominion
Virginia, USA

10

7
95 mph (152.9kph)
Steel Dragon 2000
Nagashima Spa Land
Mie, Japan

11

85 mph (136.7kph)
Goliath Phantom's Revenge
Six Flags Magic Mountain
California, USA

Titan
Kennywood
Pennsylvania, USA
and
Six Flags over Texas
Texas, USA

Indispensable soaps

The world's longest-running television soap operas still in production and their launch dates

Coronation Street
UK
1960

General Hospital
USA
1963

Days of Our Lives
USA
1965

Emmerdale
UK
1972

The Young and the Restless
USA
1973

People of the Valley
UK (Wales)
1974

Neighbours
Australia
1985

Lime Street
Germany
1985

Eastenders
UK
1985

Coffee Shop
Sri Lanka
1987

The Bold and the Beautiful
USA
1987

Home and Away
Australia
1988

Fair City
Ireland
1989

Good Times, Bad Times
Netherlands
1990

Familie
Belgium
1991

Shortland Street
New Zealand
1992

Good Times, Bad Times
Germany
1994

Among Us
Germany
1994

Royal Palm Estate
Jamaica
1994

Generations
South Africa
1994

Upper Street
Spain
1994

Malhação
Brazil
1995

Kotikatu
Finland
1995

Ros na Rún
Ireland
1995

Hollyoaks
UK
1995

Round and Round
UK (Wales)
1995

Virginie
Canada
1996

A Place in the Sun
Italy
1996

Klan
Poland
1997

Among Friends
Hungary
1998

Hotel Caesar
Norway
1998

Isidingo
South Africa
1998

Murhango
South Africa
1998

Odds of dying

The most common causes of death in the USA

Heart disease—1 in 6

Cancer—1 in 7

Stroke—1 in 28

Motor vehicle accident—1 in 88

Intentional self-harm—1 in 112

Accidental poisoning—1 in 130

Falls—1 in 171

Assault by firearm—1 in 306

Being a pedestrian—1 in 649

Motorbike riding—1 in 770

Accidental drowning—1 in 1,123

Exposure to smoke and fire—1 in 1,177

Cycling—1 in 4,717

Air and space transport—1 in 7,032

Cataclysmic storm—1 in 46,044

Fireworks—1 in 386,766

Born to yawn

Who are the most bored people in the world?

The boredom factor indicates the percentage of respondents in each country who reported feeling bored the previous day in a survey

Country	Boredom factor
Netherlands	9.5
Belgium	11.5
Austria	11.6
Denmark	12.3
Slovenia	12.8
Germany	13.7
Brazil	13.9
Switzerland	14.2
Czech Republic	14.9
France	16.0
Portugal	16.2
Slovakia	16.8
Estonia	17.6
Finland	18.1
Russia	18.7
Sweden	19.0
Australia	20.3
Spain	20.8

Country	Value
China	21.4
India	21.5
Ireland	21.6
Japan	21.8
South Africa	22.0
Norway	22.2
Poland	22.3
Canada	22.4
Italy	23.7
New Zealand	24.0
UK	27.1
Greece	29.1
South Korea	29.7
USA	29.8
Chile	30.6
Mexico	30.8
Israel	31.3
Indonesia	31.8

Pack of 20

Cigarette prices worldwide (USD)

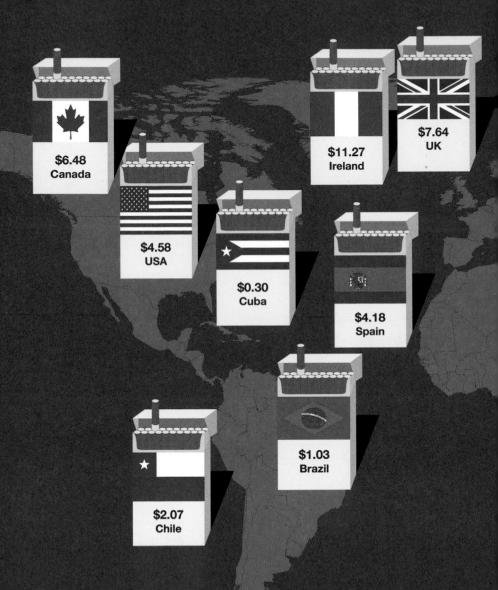

$6.48
Canada

$4.58
USA

$0.30
Cuba

$11.27
Ireland

$7.64
UK

$4.18
Spain

$1.03
Brazil

$2.07
Chile

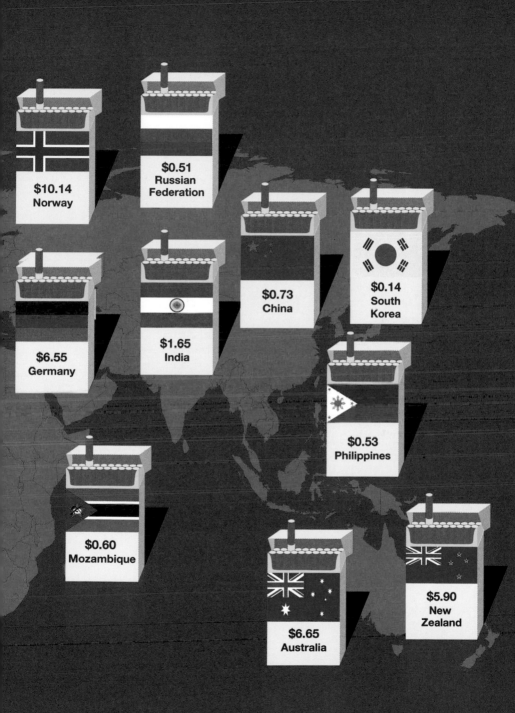

$10.14
Norway

$0.51
Russian
Federation

$6.55
Germany

$1.65
India

$0.73
China

$0.14
South
Korea

$0.53
Philippines

$0.60
Mozambique

$6.65
Australia

$5.90
New
Zealand

Shopping cities

The retail area of the world's biggest
shopping malls in terms of the equivalent
number of soccer pitches

Soccer
pitch size

$117,000$sq ft / $10,800$m^2

61

South China Mall
Dongguan, China
Opened 2005
7.1 million sq ft / 660,000m^2

52

Golden Resources Shopping Mall
Beijing, China
Opened 2004
6.0 million sq ft / 560,000m^2

36

SM Mall of Asia
Pasay City, Philippines
Opened 2006
4.2 million sq ft / 386,000m^2

32

Dubai Mall
Dubai, United Arab Emirates
Opened 2008
3.8 million sq ft / 350,000m^2

32

West Edmonton mall
Edmonton, Alberta, Canada
Opened 1981
3.8 million sq ft / 350,000m^2

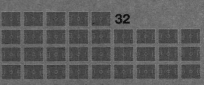

32

Cevahir Istanbul
Istanbul, Turkey
Opened 2005
3.8 million sq ft / 348,000m^2

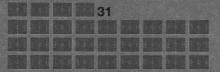 31

SM City North Edsa
Quezon City, Philippines
Opened 1985
3.6 million sq ft / 332,000m^2

 30

Beijing Mall
Beijing, China
Opened 2005
3.4 million sq ft / 320,000m^2

 26

Zhengjia Plaza
Guangzhou, China
Opened 2005
3.0 million sq ft / 280,000m^2

 24

Mall of America
Bloomington, Minnesota, USA
Opened 1992
2.8 million sq ft / 260,000m^2

 23

South Coast Plaza
Costa Mesa, California, USA
Opened 1967
2.7 million sq ft / 250,000m^2

 31

SM Megamall
Mandaluyong City, Philippines
Opened 1991
3.6 million sq ft / 332,000m^2

 30

Berjaya Times Square
Kuala Lumpur, Malaysia
Opened 2005
3.4 million sq ft / 320,000m^2

 25

SM City
Cebu City, Philippines
Opened 1991
2.9 million sq ft / 267,000m^2

 23

Central Commercial Santafe
Bogotá, Colombia
Opened 2006
2.7 million sq ft / 250,000m^2

 23

Central World Plaza
Bangkok, Thailand
Opened 2006
2.6 million sq ft / 244,000m^2

Let no man put asunder

The world's most expensive divorce settlements (USD)

$1.7 billion
Rupert & Anna
Murdoch
1999

$1–1.2 billion
Bernie & Slavica
Ecclestone
2009

$874 million
Adnan & Soraya
Khashoggi
1982

$741 million
Stephen & Elaine
Wynn
2009

$460 million +
Craig & Wendy
McCaw
1998

$400 million
Robert & Sheila
Johnson
2010

$188–376 million
Paul McCartney
& Heather Mills
2008

$300 million
Roman & Irina
Abramovich
2007

$184 million
Michael & Maya
Polsky
2008

$168 million
Michael & Juanita
Vanoy Jordan
2006

$150 million
Neil Diamond
& Marcia Murphey
1994

$100–110 million
Tiger Woods &
Elin Nordegren
2010

$103 million
Greg Norman &
Laura Andrassy
2008

$100 million
Steven Spielberg
& Amy Irving
1989

$100 million
Harrison & Melissa
Mathieson
1989

$76–92 million
Madonna
& Guy Ritchie
2008

$80 million
Kevin Costner
& Cindy Silva
1994

$60 million
Kenny & Marianne
Rogers
1993

$50 million
James Cameron
& Linda Hamilton
1999

$45 million
Michael & Diandra
Douglas
1997

$30 million
Ted Danson
& Casey Coates
1993

$25 million
Mick Jagger
& Jerry Hall
1999

87

World stadia

The world's sports stadia with a capacity over 100,000, listed with location and sport

Capacity	Name of stadium	Country	Sport
250,000	Indianapolis Speedway	USA	🏎
223,000	Tokyo Racecourse	Japan	🏇
200,000	Shanghai Int'l Circuit	China	🏎
168,000	Daytona Int'l Speedway	USA	🏎
167,000	Charlotte Motor Speedway	USA	🏎
165,676	Nakayama Racecourse	Japan	🏇
160,000	Bristol Motor Speedway	USA	🏎
155,000	Suzuka Circuit	Japan	🏎
155,000	Istanbul Park	Turkey	🏎
154,861	Texas Motor Speedway	USA	🏎
150,000	Rungrado May Day Stadium	N. Korea	🏁
150,000	Nürburgring	Germany	🏎
143,000	Talladega Superspeedway	USA	🏎
140,700	Circuit de Catalunya	Spain	🏎
140,700	Dover Int'l Speedway	USA	🏎
140,700	Las Vegas Motor Speedway	USA	🏎
139,877	Hanshin Racecourse	Japan	🏇
137,000	Autodromo di Monza	Italy	🏎
136,373	Michigan Int'l Speedway	USA	🏎
135,000	Korea International Circuit	S. Korea	🏎
130,000	Flemington Racecourse	Australia	🏇
124,000	Atlanta Motor Speedway	USA	🏎
120,000	Saltlake Stadium	India	⚽

KEY

🎡 Motor racing   🏈 American football   🚩 National stadium

Ω Horse racing   ⚽ Soccer   ⚫ Multiuse

Capacity	Name of stadium	Country	Sport
120,000	Kyoto Racecourse	Japan	Ω
120,000	Hockenheimring	Germany	🎡
120,000	EuroSpeedway Lausitz	Germany	🎡
120,000	Circuit Ricardo Tormo	Spain	🎡
120,000	Churchill Downs	USA	Ω
109,901	Michigan Stadium	USA	🏈
107,282	Beaver Stadium	USA	🏈
105,064	Estadio Azteca	Mexico	⚽
105,000	Richmond Int'l Raceway	USA	🎡
102,329	Ohio Stadium	USA	🏈
102,037	Neyland Stadium	USA	🏈
101,821	Bryant Denny Stadium	USA	🏈
100,200	Bukit Jalil Stadium	Malaysia	🚩
100,119	DKR-Texas Memorial Stadium	USA	🏈
100,000	Bung Karno Stadium	Indonesia	🚩
100,000	Circuit Bugatti	France	🎡
100,000	TT Circuit Assen	Netherlands	🎡
100,000	Autódromo do Algarve	Portugal	🎡
100,000	Azadi Stadium	Iran	⚽
100,000	Circuit Gilles Villeneuve	Canada	🎡
100,000	Autódromo H. Rodríguez	Mexico	🎡
100,000	Melbourne Cricket Ground	Australia	⚫
100,000	Hipódromo de San Isidro	Argentina	Ω

Much hairdo...

Iconic hairstyles of the 20th century

Bob

Mullet

Dreadlocks

Quiff

Perm

Mohawk

The "Rachel"

Beehive

The "Veronica Lake"

The "Jackie O"

The "Farrah Fawcett"

Pompadour

Poodle Cut

The "Grace Kelly"

Bouffant

The "Marilyn"

Bettie Page fringe

Afro

Updo

Twiggy crop

Top knot

Feed the world

Developing and transition countries ranked according to three combined hunger indicators: population undernourishment, number of underweight children under five, and child mortality rate

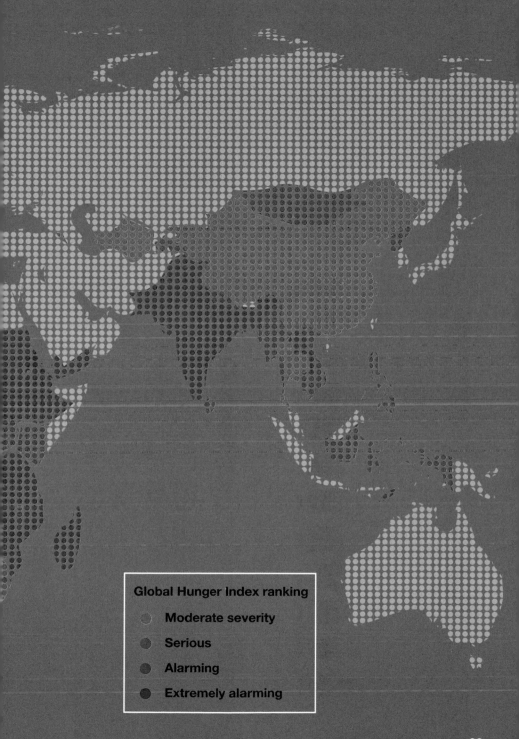

Global Hunger Index ranking

- Moderate severity
- Serious
- Alarming
- Extremely alarming

93

Sting index

The world's most venomous land snakes, ranked by their LD_{50} (median lethal dose): the quantity of venom in milligrams per kilogram of body mass of the subject which if injected would result in the death of 50% of those tested within a given time frame

1.

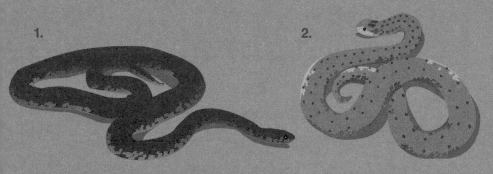

INLAND TAIPAN
0.025 mg

2.

EASTERN BROWN SNAKE
0.0365 mg

3.

COASTAL TAIPAN
0.106 mg

4.

MANY-BANDED KRAIT
0.108 mg

94

5.

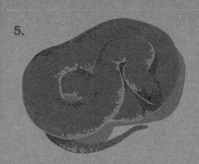

PENINSULA TIGER SNAKE
0.131 mg

6.

SAW-SCALED VIPER
0.151 mg

7.

BLACK MAMBA
0.185 mg

8.

WESTERN TIGER SNAKE
0.194 mg

9.

EASTERN CORAL SNAKE
0.196 mg

10.

PHILIPPINE COBRA
0.20 mg

Extended lives

Increases in national life expectancy from
1950–55 to 2005–10

Countries with lowest increase

	1950–55		2005–10
Zimbabwe	48		46
Ukraine	66		67
Russia	64		67
Belarus	65		69
Lesotho	42		46
Zambia	42		46
Botswana	47		53
Swaziland	41		47
South Africa	45		51
Latvia	66		72

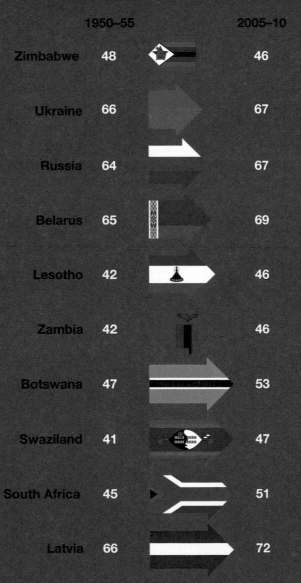

KEY

Life expectancy in years of those born in 1950–55: 64

Life expectancy in years of those born in 2005–10: 67

Countries with highest increase

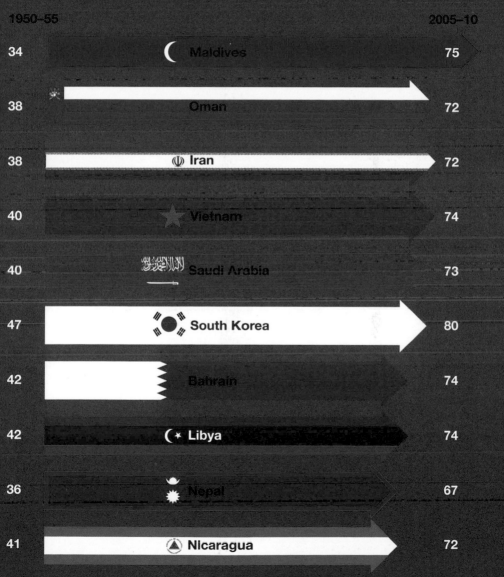

1950–55	Country	2005–10
34	Maldives	75
38	Oman	72
38	Iran	72
40	Vietnam	74
40	Saudi Arabia	73
47	South Korea	80
42	Bahrain	74
42	Libya	74
36	Nepal	67
41	Nicaragua	72

Leap into oblivion

The world's longest bungee jumps

467 ft / 142m
Navajo Bridges, Marble Canyon, Arizona, USA

486ft / 148m
Perrine Bridge, Twin Falls, Idaho, USA

500ft / 152m
Ponte Colossus, Italy

524ft / 160m
Bhote Kosi River, Himalayas, Nepal

623ft / 190m
Niouc, Switzerland

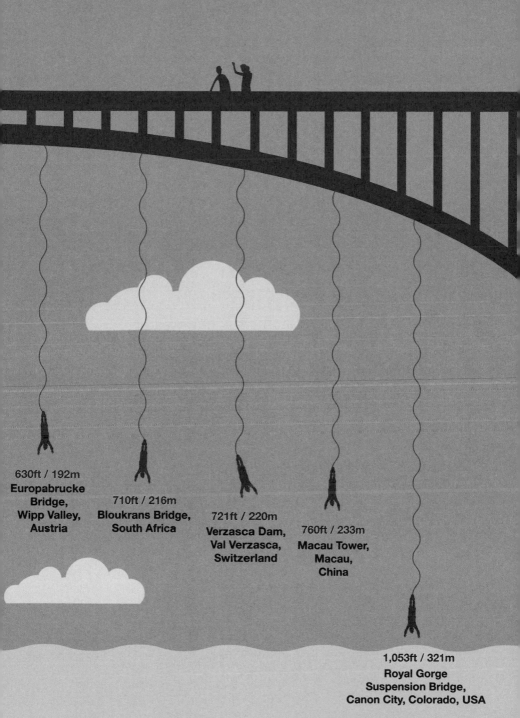

630ft / 192m
Europabrucke Bridge, Wipp Valley, Austria

710ft / 216m
Bloukrans Bridge, South Africa

721ft / 220m
Verzasca Dam, Val Verzasca, Switzerland

760ft / 233m
Macau Tower, Macau, China

1,053ft / 321m
Royal Gorge Suspension Bridge, Canon City, Colorado, USA

99

Learning abroad

Number of foreign students studying in countries around the world

Canada **93,479**

Germany **180,135**

USA **660,581**

Finland **10,980**

Denmark **12,582**

Ireland **12,937**

Hungary **14,518**

Poland **16,976**

Netherlands **23,674**

Sweden **27,040**

Belgium **33,991**

Switzerland **34,847**

New Zealand **38,350**

Austria **46,545**

Spain **48,517**

Japan **119,626**

Australia **257,637**

UK **368,968**

Source: Based on data from OECD (2011), 'Education Database: Foreign/international students enrolled', OECD Education Statistics (database)

Uniting nations

The number of days spent in each foreign country visited by the UN Secretary-General Ban Ki-moon during official visits in 2011

UN HEADQUARTERS NEW YORK

LI

TUNISIA
3

COLOMBIA
3

GUATEMALA
3

ECUADOR
2

CÔTE D'IVOIRE
2

NIGER
3

BRAZIL
4

PERU
3

URUGUAY
2

ARGENTINA
2

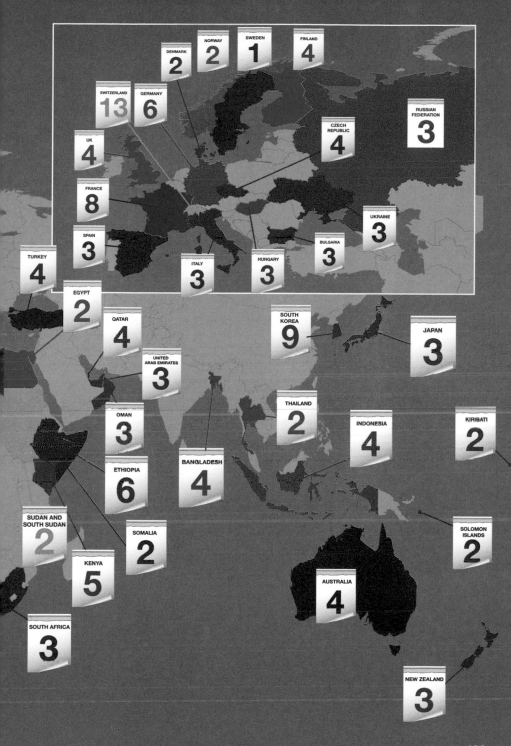

DENMARK 2
NORWAY 2
SWEDEN 1
FINLAND 4
SWITZERLAND 13
GERMANY 6
RUSSIAN FEDERATION 3
CZECH REPUBLIC 4
UK 4
FRANCE 8
UKRAINE 3
SPAIN 3
ITALY 3
HUNGARY 3
BULGARIA 3
TURKEY 4
EGYPT 2
QATAR 4
SOUTH KOREA 9
JAPAN 3
UNITED ARAB EMIRATES 3
THAILAND 2
INDONESIA 4
KIRIBATI 2
OMAN 3
BANGLADESH 4
ETHIOPIA 6
SOLOMON ISLANDS 2
SUDAN AND SOUTH SUDAN 2
SOMALIA 2
KENYA 5
AUSTRALIA 4
SOUTH AFRICA 3
NEW ZEALAND 3

Boxing home towns

Home towns of US Heavyweight World Boxing champions since World War II and the year they first won the title

Joe Louis **Lafayette, Alabama, 1937**
Ezzard Charles **Lawrenceville, Georgia, 1949**
Jersey Joe Walcott **Merchantville, New Jersey, 1951**
Rocky Marciano **Brockton, Massachusetts, 1952**
Floyd Patterson **Waco, North Carolina, 1956**
Sonny Liston **St Francis County, Arkansas, 1962**
Cassius Clay/Muhammad Ali **Louisville, Kentucky, 1964**
Ernie Terrell **Belzoni, Mississippi, 1965**
Joe Frazier **Beaufort, South Carolina, 1968**
Jimmy Ellis **Louisville, Kentucky, 1968**
George Foreman **Marshall, Texas, 1973**
Leon Spinks **St Louis, Missouri, 1978**
Ken Norton **Jacksonville, Illinois, 1978**
Larry Holmes **Cuthbert, Georgia, 1978**
John Tate **Marion, Arkansas, 1979**
Mike Weaver **Gatesville, Texas, 1980**
Michael Dokes **Akron, Ohio, 1982**
Tim Witherspoon **Philadelphia, Pennsylvania, 1984**
Pinklon Thomas **Pontiac, Michigan, 1984**

Greg Page Louisville, Kentucky, 1984
Tony Tubbs Cincinnati, Ohio, 1985
Mike Spinks St Louis, Missouri, 1985
Mike Tyson Brooklyn, NYC, 1986
James Smith Magnolia, North Carolina, 1986
Tony Tucker Grand Rapids, Michigan, 1987
Buster Douglas Columbus, Ohio, 1990
Evander Holyfield Atmore, Alabama, 1990
Ray Mercer Jacksonville, Florida, 1991
Michael Moorer Monessen, Pennsylvania, 1992
Riddick Bowe Brooklyn, NYC, 1992
Tommy Morrison Gravette, Arkansas, 1993
Bruce Seldon Atlantic City, New Jersey, 1995
Chris Byrd Flint, Michigan, 2000
John Ruiz Methuen, Massachusetts, 2001
Roy Jones Jnr Pensacola, Florida, 2003
Lamon Brewster Indianapolis, Indiana, 2004
Hasim Rahman Baltimore, Maryland, 2005
Shannon Briggs Brooklyn, NYC, 2006

Copper index

The number of police officers
per 100,000 population

Italy 553

Mexico 486

Greece 435

MEAN 356
Israel 330
Ireland 306
Hungary 284
UK 263

USA 224
South Africa 220
Canada 191
New Zealand 187

India 122

Kuwait 1,065

Northern Ireland 528

Spain 475

Singapore 396

France 345

Germany 304

Colombia 229
Australia 222
Japan 200
Chile 188

Finland 154

Kenya 99

Revolutionary fervor

Popular uprisings with unusual names in the last 100 years

 Easter Uprising
1916—Dublin, Ireland (it happened at Easter)

 Green Corn Rebellion
1917—Oklahoma, USA (the rebels were going to march across the country eating green corn for sustenance)

 Pitchfork Uprising
1920—Tatarstan, Russia (after the weapons the peasants had)

 The Rosewater Revolution
1952—Lebanon (bloodless peaceful revolution)

 The Carnation Revolution
1974—Portugal (population put carnations in revolutionaries' guns)

 The Yellow Revolution
1986—Philippines (yellow ribbons used by supporters)

 The 8888 Uprising
1988—Myanmar (key events happened 08/08/88)

 The Velvet Revolution
1989—Czechoslovakia (peaceful revolution)

 The Log Revolution
1990—Croatia (blockades made from logs)

 The Bulldozer Revolution
2000—Yugoslavia (after a vehicle driven into Serbian Television building)

The Rose Revolution

2003—Georgia (supporters burst into Parliament with roses in their hands)

 The Orange Revolution

2004—Ukraine (color of opposition party)

 The Blue Revolution

2005—Kuwait (color used by protesters in favor of women's suffrage)

 The Purple Revolution

2005—Iraq (ink color used to identify voters)

 The Cedar Revolution

2005—Lebanon (named after the national symbol of Lebanon)

 The Tulip Revolution

2005—Kyrgyzstan (term used by the incumbent president who was then overthrown)

 The Green Movement

2009—Iran (color of one opposition party's campaign)

 The Kitchenware Revolution

2009—Iceland (protesters banged together pots and pans in demonstrations)

 The Jasmine Revolution

2010—Tunisia (Tunisia's national flower)

 The Lotus Revolution

2011—Egypt (flower highly prized by ancient Egyptians)

Fast service

The fastest recorded tennis serves since 1990 by male professional players

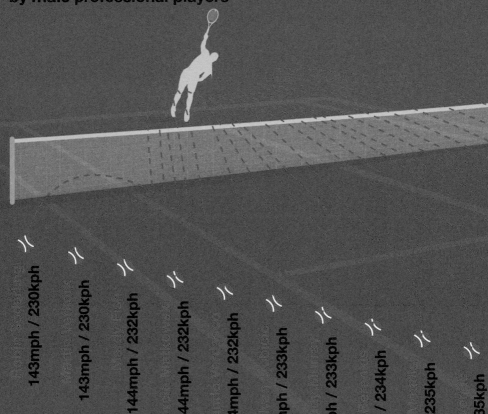

143mph / 230kph

143mph / 230kph

144mph / 232kph

144mph / 232kph

144mph / 232kph

145mph / 233kph

145mph / 233kph

145.4mph / 234kph

146mph / 235kph

146mph / 235kph

146.8mph / 236kph

149mph / 240kph

149.3mph / 240kph

149.8mph / 241kph

149.9mph / 241kph

152mph / 245kph

155mph / 249kph

155mph / 249kph

156mph / 251kph

163mph / 262kph

The premature dead

Untimely deaths of rock legends

Ritchie Valens, 17
Plane crash
1959

Eddie Cochrane, 21
Traffic accident
1960

Sid Vicious, 21
Booze and pills
1979

Buddy Holly, 22
Plane crash
1959

Ian Curtis, 23
Suicide
1980

Notorious B.I.G., 24
Murder
1997

Tupac Shakur, 25
Murder
1996

Jimi Hendrix, 27
Booze and pills
1970

Brian Jones, 27
**Drowned in
swimming pool
1969**

Janis Joplin, 27
Heroin overdose
1970

Jim Morrison, 27
In the bathtub
1971

Amy Winehouse, 27
Alcohol
2011

112

Tim Buckley, 28
**Heroin overdose
1975**

Otis Redding, 26
**Plane crash
1967**

JP "The Big Bopper"
Richardson, 28
**Plane crash
1959**

Marc Bolan, 29
**Car crash
1977**

Jeff Buckley, 30
**Drowned
1997**

Keith Moon, 31
**Prescription drugs
1978**

John Bonham, 32
**Alcohol—
40 shots of vodka
1980**

Sam Cooke, 33
**Shot by
motel owner
1964**

Gene Vincent, 36
**Stomach ulcer
1971**

Michael Hutchence, 37
**Suicide
1997**

Dennis Wilson, 39
**Drowned
1983**

John Lennon, 40
**Shot
1980**

Elvis Presley, 42
**Prescription drugs
1977**

Marvin Gaye, 44
**Shot by father
1984**

Whitney
Houston, 48
**In the bathtub
2012**

Michael Jackson, 50
**Prescription drugs
2009**

113

Union power

Percentage of salaried workforce who belong to a trade union

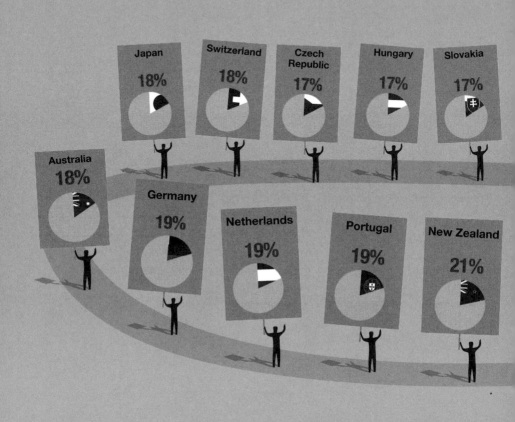

Japan 18%

Switzerland 18%

Czech Republic 17%

Hungary 17%

Slovakia 17%

Australia 18%

Germany 19%

Netherlands 19%

Portugal 19%

New Zealand 21%

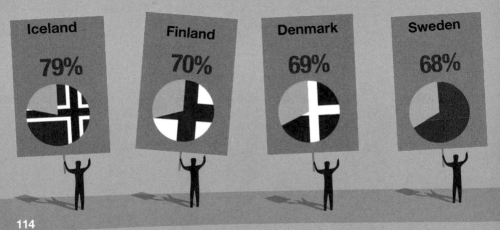

Iceland 79%

Finland 70%

Denmark 69%

Sweden 68%

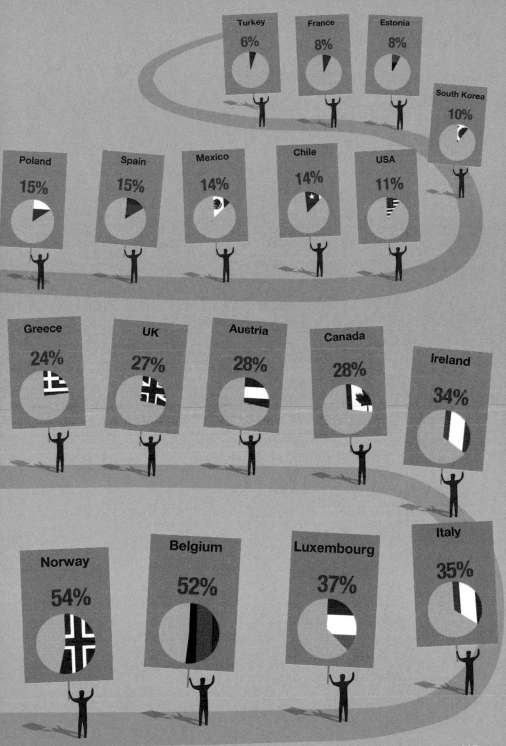

Turkey 6%

France 8%

Estonia 8%

South Korea 10%

Poland 15%

Spain 15%

Mexico 14%

Chile 14%

USA 11%

Greece 24%

UK 27%

Austria 28%

Canada 28%

Ireland 34%

Norway 54%

Belgium 52%

Luxembourg 37%

Italy 35%

McWorld

Countries with the most McDonalds restaurants worldwide

1	USA	14,027		11	Italy	410
2	Japan	3,302		12	Mexico	397
3	Canada	1,434		13	Taiwan	348
4	Germany	1,386		14	Philippines	309
5	China	1,287		15	Russia	275
6	UK	1,194		16	Poland	258
7	France	1,193		17	South Korea	242
8	Australia	831		18	Sweden	229
9	Brazil	616		19	Hong Kong	226
10	Spain	414		20	Netherlands	225

117

The millionaire's shopping basket

Each year *Forbes* magazine publishes the CLEWI (Cost of Living Extremely Well Index) of 40 items that are essential for luxury living. Here's what's on the list (USD):

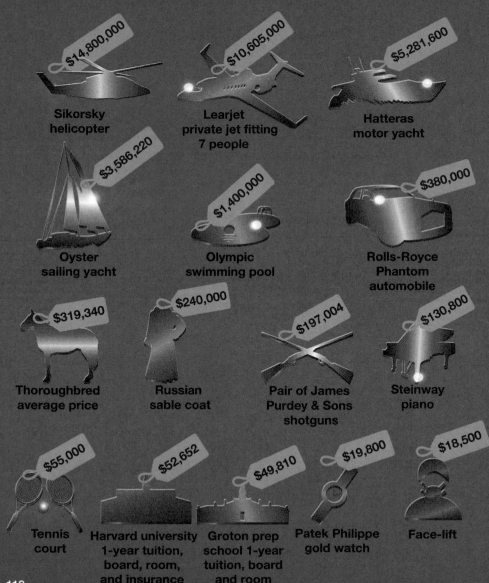

$14,800,000 — Sikorsky helicopter

$10,605,000 — Learjet private jet fitting 7 people

$5,281,600 — Hatteras motor yacht

$3,586,220 — Oyster sailing yacht

$1,400,000 — Olympic swimming pool

$380,000 — Rolls-Royce Phantom automobile

$319,340 — Thoroughbred average price

$240,000 — Russian sable coat

$197,004 — Pair of James Purdey & Sons shotguns

$130,800 — Steinway piano

$55,000 — Tennis court

$52,652 — Harvard university 1-year tuition, board, room, and insurance

$49,810 — Groton prep school 1-year tuition, board and room

$19,800 — Patek Philippe gold watch

$18,500 — Face-lift

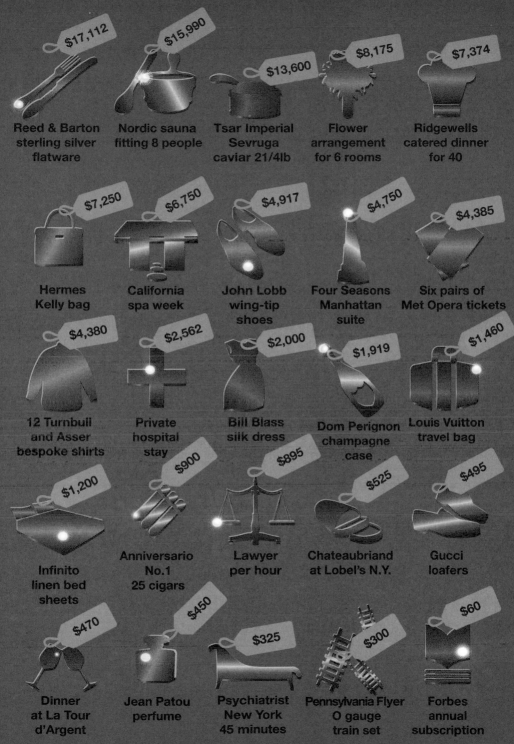

$17,112 — Reed & Barton sterling silver flatware

$15,990 — Nordic sauna fitting 8 people

$13,600 — Tsar Imperial Sevruga caviar 2 1/4lb

$8,175 — Flower arrangement for 6 rooms

$7,374 — Ridgewells catered dinner for 40

$7,250 — Hermes Kelly bag

$6,750 — California spa week

$4,917 — John Lobb wing-tip shoes

$4,750 — Four Seasons Manhattan suite

$4,385 — Six pairs of Met Opera tickets

$4,380 — 12 Turnbull and Asser bespoke shirts

$2,562 — Private hospital stay

$2,000 — Bill Blass silk dress

$1,919 — Dom Perignon champagne case

$1,460 — Louis Vuitton travel bag

$1,200 — Infinito linen bed sheets

$900 — Anniversario No.1 25 cigars

$895 — Lawyer per hour

$525 — Chateaubriand at Lobel's N.Y.

$495 — Gucci loafers

$470 — Dinner at La Tour d'Argent

$450 — Jean Patou perfume

$325 — Psychiatrist New York 45 minutes

$300 — Pennsylvania Flyer O gauge train set

$60 — Forbes annual subscription

Vacation money

The highest and lowest earnings from tourism on a per capita basis (in USD) around the world

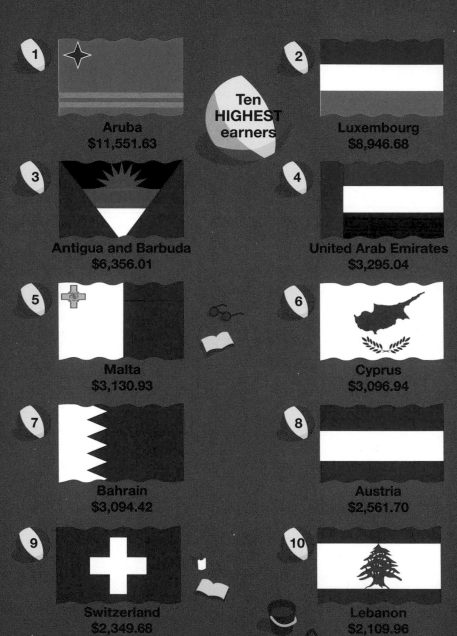

Ten HIGHEST earners

1. Aruba
$11,551.63

2. Luxembourg
$8,946.68

3. Antigua and Barbuda
$6,356.01

4. United Arab Emirates
$3,295.04

5. Malta
$3,130.93

6. Cyprus
$3,096.94

7. Bahrain
$3,094.42

8. Austria
$2,561.70

9. Switzerland
$2,349.68

10. Lebanon
$2,109.96

120

Ten LOWEST earners

1. Guinea $0.21
2. Bangladesh $0.70
3. Sudan $2.28
4. Sierra Leone $4.33
5. Tajikistan $4.43
6. Nigeria $5.27
7. Pakistan $6.02
8. Cameroon $6.75
9. Zambia $10.87
10. Mozambique $11.56

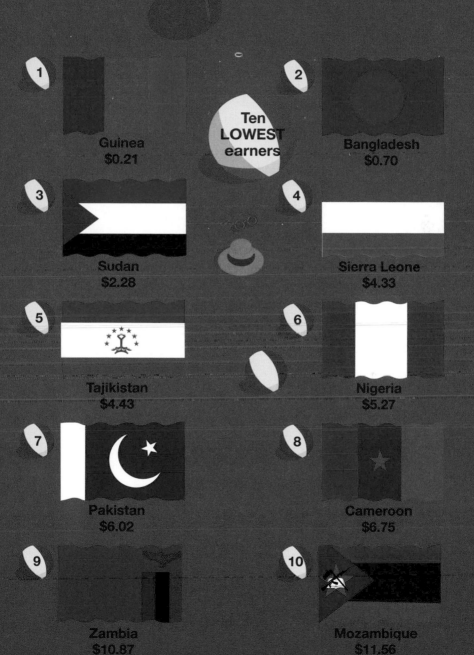

What's it worth?

The insurance valuations of the body parts of the rich and famous (USD)

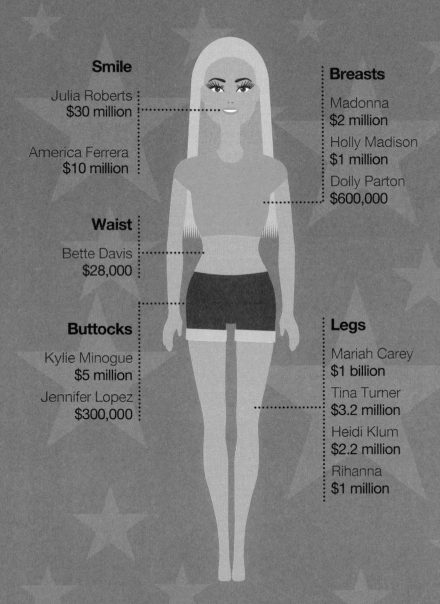

Smile

Julia Roberts
$30 million

America Ferrera
$10 million

Breasts

Madonna
$2 million

Holly Madison
$1 million

Dolly Parton
$600,000

Waist

Bette Davis
$28,000

Buttocks

Kylie Minogue
$5 million

Jennifer Lopez
$300,000

Legs

Mariah Carey
$1 billion

Tina Turner
$3.2 million

Heidi Klum
$2.2 million

Rihanna
$1 million

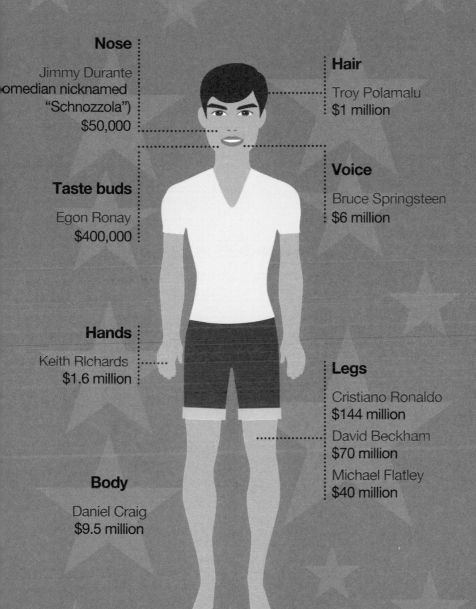

Nose

Jimmy Durante
(comedian nicknamed "Schnozzola")
$50,000

Hair

Troy Polamalu
$1 million

Taste buds

Egon Ronay
$400,000

Voice

Bruce Springsteen
$6 million

Hands

Keith Richards
$1.6 million

Legs

Cristiano Ronaldo
$144 million

David Beckham
$70 million

Michael Flatley
$40 million

Body

Daniel Craig
$9.5 million

123

Byte race

Speed of the most powerful computer processors 1971–present

1971: **0.092 MIPS**

1979: **1.0 MIPS**

1982: **2.66 MIPS**

1984: **4.0 MIPS**

1974–77: **0.5 MIPS**

1985: **11.4 MIPS**

1994: **188 MIPS**

1996: **541 MIPS**

1992: **54 MIPS**

1999: **2,054 MIPS**

1990: **44 MIPS**

2000: **3,561 MIPS**

• =10 MIPS (million instructions per second)

a single dot expanded to show earliest speeds

2003: **9,726 MIPS**

2005: **19,200 MIPS**

2006: **49,161 MIPS**

2008: **82,300 MIPS**

2010: **147,600 MIPS**

present: **177,730 MIPS**

White House wallets

The personal wealth of the richest presidential candidates over the past 20 years (USD)

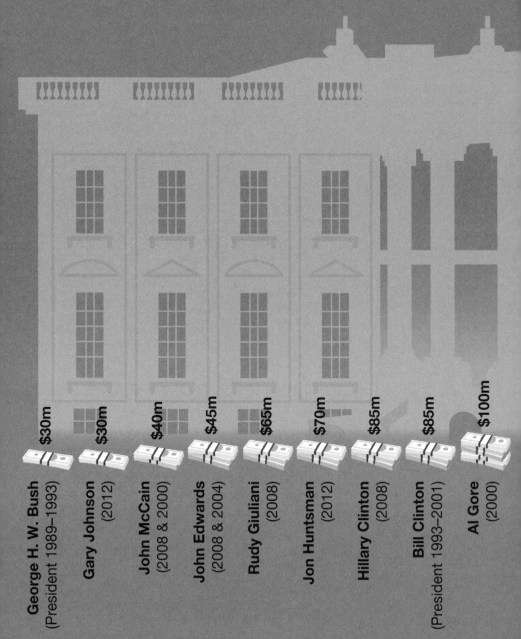

$30m — George H. W. Bush (President 1989–1993)

$30m — Gary Johnson (2012)

$40m — John McCain (2008 & 2000)

$45m — John Edwards (2008 & 2004)

$65m — Rudy Giuliani (2008)

$70m — Jon Huntsman (2012)

$85m — Hillary Clinton (2008)

$85m — Bill Clinton (President 1993–2001)

$100m — Al Gore (2000)

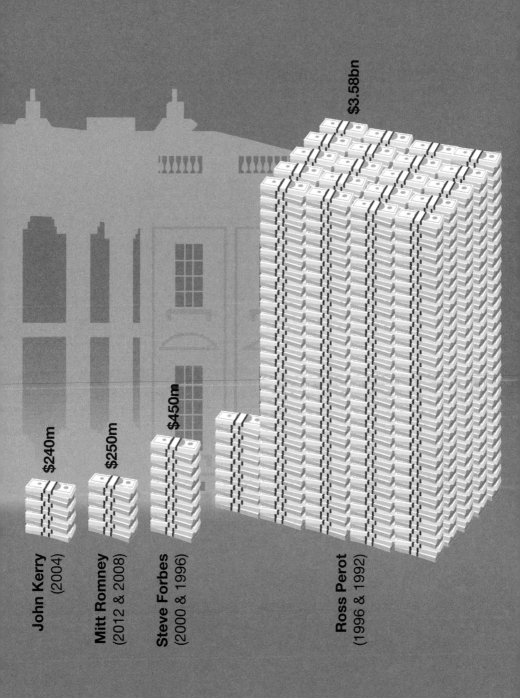

$3.58bn

$450m

$250m

$240m

John Kerry
(2004)

Mitt Romney
(2012 & 2008)

Steve Forbes
(2000 & 1996)

Ross Perot
(1996 & 1992)

Book lovers

Number of books published annually in different countries per million of population

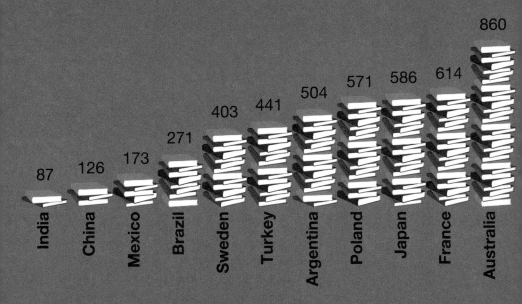

Country	Value
India	87
China	126
Mexico	173
Brazil	271
Sweden	403
Turkey	441
Argentina	504
Poland	571
Japan	586
France	614
Australia	860

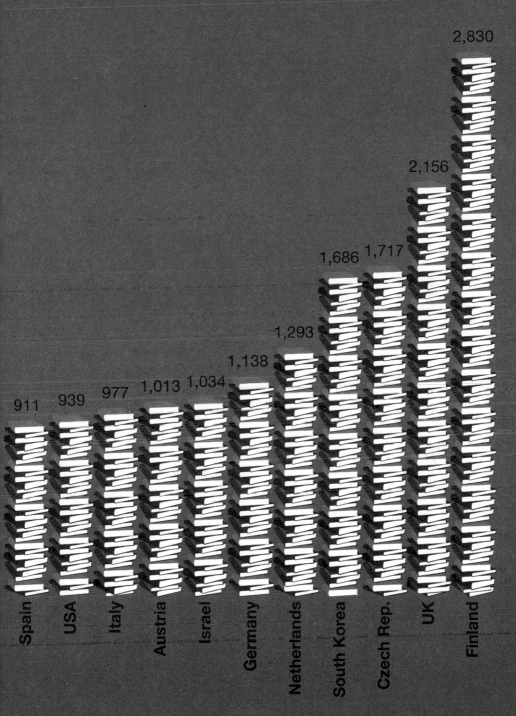

Spain 911
USA 939
Italy 977
Austria 1,013
Israel 1,034
Germany 1,138
Netherlands 1,293
South Korea 1,686
Czech Rep. 1,717
UK 2,156
Finland 2,830

Shore thing

Countries with the most Blue Flag awards for clean beaches

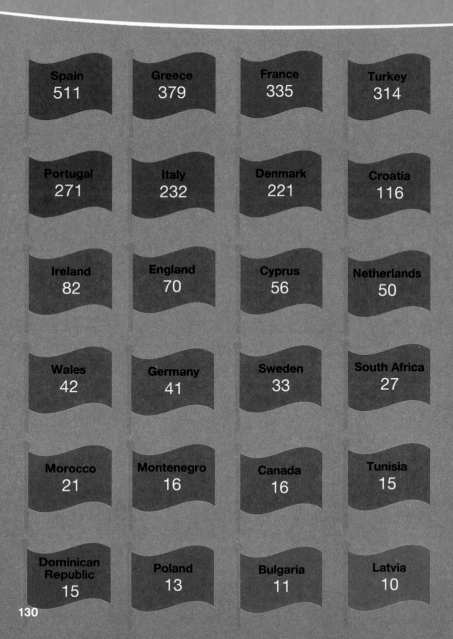

Spain	511
Greece	379
France	335
Turkey	314
Portugal	271
Italy	232
Denmark	221
Croatia	116
Ireland	82
England	70
Cyprus	56
Netherlands	50
Wales	42
Germany	41
Sweden	33
South Africa	27
Morocco	21
Montenegro	16
Canada	16
Tunisia	15
Dominican Republic	15
Poland	13
Bulgaria	11
Latvia	10

Jamaica 8	Slovenia 7	Scotland 7	Puerto Rico 7
Northern Ireland 7	Norway 6	Ukraine 5	US Virgin Islands 4
New Zealand 3	Lithuania 3	Jordan 3	Turks & Caicos Islands 3
United Arab Emirates 2	Malta 2	Sint Maarten 1	Romania 1
Iceland 1	Brazil 1	Russia 0	

The order of fangs

Top 50 highest-grossing vampire movies at the US Box Office

1
$300.5m
The Twilight Saga: Eclipse (2010)

2
$296.5m
The Twilight Saga: New Moon (2009)

3
$281m
The Twilight Saga: Breaking Dawn Part 1 (2011)

4
$193m
Twilight (2008)

5
$120m
Van Helsing (2004)

6
$105m
Interview with the Vampire (1994)

7
$82.5m
Bram Stoker's Dracula (1992)

8
$82.3m
Blade II (2002)

9
$79.6m
Dark Shadows (2012)

10
$70m
Blade (1998)

11
$62.3m
Underworld Awakening (2012)

12
$62.3m
Underworld: Evolution (2006)

13
$52.4m
Blade: Trinity (2004)

14
$52m
Underworld (2003)

15
$45.8m
Underworld: Rise of the Lycans (2009)

16
$43.9m
Love at First Bite (1979)

17
$39.6m
30 Days of Night (2007)

18
$37m
Abraham Lincoln: Vampire Hunter (2012)

19
$36.7m
Vampires Suck (2010)

20
$33m
Dracula 2000 (2000)

21
$32.2m
The Lost Boys (1987)

22
$30.3m
Queen of the Damned (2002)

23
$30.1m
Daybreakers (2010)

24
$29.1m
Priest (2011)

25
$25.8m
From Dusk Till Dawn (1996)

26
$24.9m
Fright Night
(1985)

27
$20.3m
John
Carpenter's
Vampires
(1998)

28
$20.1m
Dracula
(1979)

29
$19.7m
Vampire in
Brooklyn
(1995)

30
$18.3m
Fright Night
(2011)

31
$16.6m
Buffy the
Vampire
Slayer
(1992)

32
$13.8m
Cirque du
Freak: The
Vampire's
Assistant
(2009)

33
$13.6m
The Little
Vampire
(2000)

34
$12.1m
Let Me In
(2010)

35
$10.8m
Dracula: Dead
and Loving It
(1995)

36
$10m
Once Bitten
(1985)

37
$8.2m
Shadow of
the Vampire
(2000)

38
$7.2m
The Forsaken
(2001)

39
$7.2m
Transylvania
6-5000
(1985)

40
$6m
The Hunger
(1983)

41
$5.8m
Bordello
of Blood
(1996)

42
$4.9m
Innocent
Blood
(1992)

43
$4.9m
Vamp
(1986)

44
$3.4m
Near Dark
(1987)

45
$3m
Fright Night II
(1989)

46
$2.4m
BloodRayne
(2006)

47
$2.2m
Def by
Temptation
(1990)

48
$2.1m
Let the Right
One In
(2008)

49
$1.2m
The Lair of
the White
Worm (1988)

50
$1.2m
Dylan Dog:
Dead of
Night (2011)

Stormy weather

The most extreme recorded weather incidents from across the world

LARGEST SNOWFLAKE EVER OBSERVED

15in (38cm) diameter
Fort Keogh, Montana, USA
January 28 1887

LARGEST WAVE

1,740ft (524m)
megatsunami
Lituya Bay, Alaska
July 9 1958

MOST RAIN IN ONE MINUTE

1.23in (31.2mm)
Unionville, Maryland, USA
July 4 1956

LEAST ANNUAL RAIN

0.0m
Death Valley,
California, USA
1929

HIGHEST ANNUAL RAINFALL

704.83in (17.903m)
Kukui, Hawaii
1982

HIGHEST
TEMPERATURE

136.0°F (57.8°C)
Aziziya, Libya, Africa
September 13 1922

HEAVIEST
HAILSTONE

2.25lb (1.0kg)
Gopalganj district, Bangladesh
April 14 1986

MOST ANNUAL
LIGHTNING STRIKES

61 per sq mile (158 per square km)
Kifuka, Democratic Republic
of the Congo

MAXIMUM
WIND GUST

253mph (113.2m/s)
Barrow Island, Australia
October 4 1996

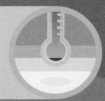

LOWEST
TEMPERATURE

−128.6°F (−89.2°C)
Vostok Station, Antarctica
July 21 1983

135

Halo halo

Canonizations during each year of the pontificate of Pope Benedict XVI, showing year and place of birth of saints

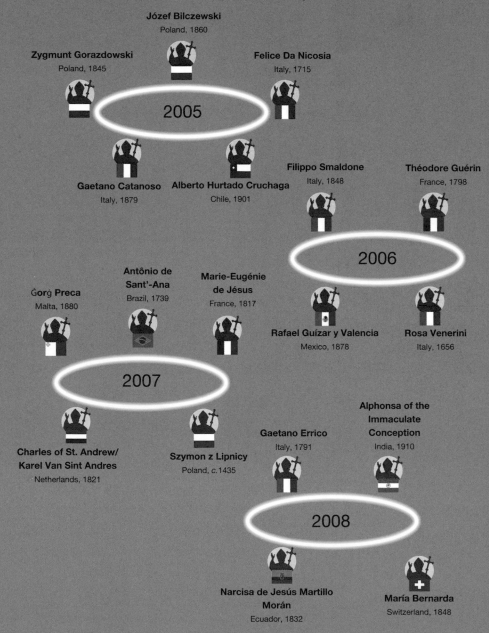

Józef Bilczewski
Poland, 1860

Zygmunt Gorazdowski
Poland, 1845

Felice Da Nicosia
Italy, 1715

2005

Gaetano Catanoso
Italy, 1879

Alberto Hurtado Cruchaga
Chile, 1901

Filippo Smaldone
Italy, 1848

Théodore Guérin
France, 1798

2006

Antônio de Sant'-Ana
Brazil, 1739

Marie-Eugénie de Jésus
France, 1817

Ġorġ Preca
Malta, 1880

Rafael Guízar y Valencia
Mexico, 1878

Rosa Venerini
Italy, 1656

2007

Charles of St. Andrew/ Karel Van Sint Andres
Netherlands, 1821

Szymon z Lipnicy
Poland, c.1435

Gaetano Errico
Italy, 1791

Alphonsa of the Immaculate Conception
India, 1910

2008

Narcisa de Jesús Martillo Morán
Ecuador, 1832

María Bernarda
Switzerland, 1848

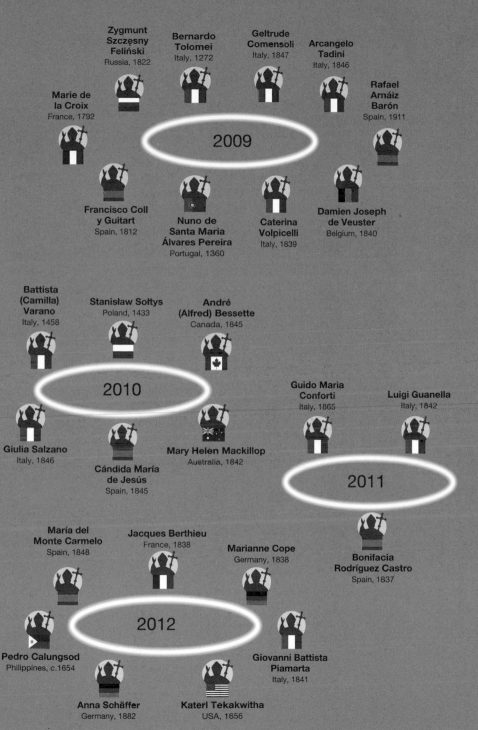

Zygmunt Szczęsny Feliński
Russia, 1822

Bernardo Tolomei
Italy, 1272

Geltrude Comensoli
Italy, 1847

Arcangelo Tadini
Italy, 1846

Marie de la Croix
France, 1792

Rafael Arnáiz Barón
Spain, 1911

2009

Francisco Coll y Guitart
Spain, 1812

Nuno de Santa Maria Álvares Pereira
Portugal, 1360

Caterina Volpicelli
Italy, 1839

Damien Joseph de Veuster
Belgium, 1840

Battista (Camilla) Varano
Italy, 1458

Stanisław Sołtys
Poland, 1433

André (Alfred) Bessette
Canada, 1845

2010

Giulia Salzano
Italy, 1846

Cándida María de Jesús
Spain, 1845

Mary Helen Mackillop
Australia, 1842

Guido Maria Conforti
Italy, 1865

Luigi Guanella
Italy, 1842

2011

María del Monte Carmelo
Spain, 1848

Jacques Berthieu
France, 1838

Marianne Cope
Germany, 1838

Bonifacia Rodríguez Castro
Spain, 1837

2012

Pedro Calungsod
Philippines, c.1654

Giovanni Battista Piamarta
Italy, 1841

Anna Schäffer
Germany, 1882

Kateri Tekakwitha
USA, 1656

I need dollars...

Average household incomes in the USA by state

$56,253 Washington

$50,526 Oregon

$47,014 Idaho

$41,467 Montana

$51,380 North Dakota

$45,669 South Dakota

$52,359 Wyoming

$52,728 Nebraska

$51,525 Nevada

$56,787 Utah

$60,442 Colorado

$46,2 Kansa

$54,459 California

$47,279 Arizona

$45,098 New Mexico

$43 Okl

$47,46 Texas

$58,507 Hawaii

$58,198 Alaska

$66,707 New Hampshire

$48,133 Maine

$55,942 Vermont

$61,333 Massachusetts

$51,914 Rhode Island

$49,826 New York

$66,452 Connecticut

$63,540 New Jersey

$55,269 Delaware

$64,025 Maryland

$55,528 District of Columbia

$50,522 Wisconsin

$46,441 Michigan

$48,460 Pennsylvania

$49,177 Iowa

$46,093 Ohio

$50,761 Illinois

$46,322 Indiana

$42,839 West Virginia

$60,363 Virginia

$46,184 Missouri

$41,236 Kentucky

$43,753 North Carolina

$38,686 Tennessee

$38,571 Arkansas

$41,709 South Carolina

Alabama $40,976

$44,108 Georgia

$37,985 Mississippi

$39,443 Louisiana

$44,243 Florida

...4 ...sota

KEY

$60,000+
$50,000–$59,000
$40,000–$49,000
$30,000–$39,000

High league

Global seizures of cannabis herb measured in tons

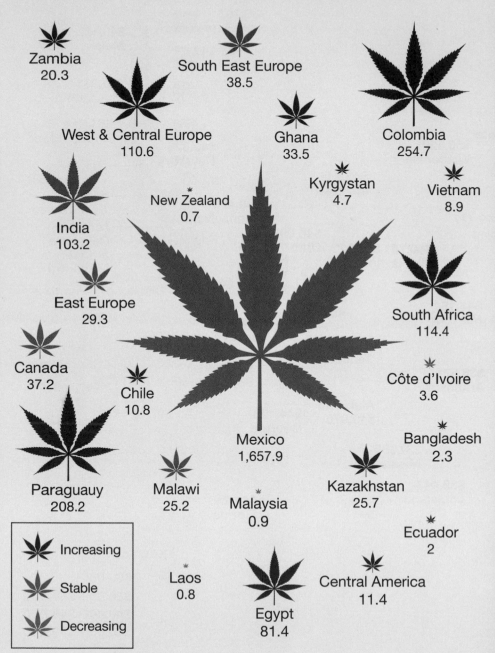

Zambia
20.3

South East Europe
38.5

West & Central Europe
110.6

Ghana
33.5

Colombia
254.7

India
103.2

New Zealand
0.7

Kyrgystan
4.7

Vietnam
8.9

East Europe
29.3

South Africa
114.4

Canada
37.2

Chile
10.8

Côte d'Ivoire
3.6

Mexico
1,657.9

Bangladesh
2.3

Paraguauy
208.2

Malawi
25.2

Malaysia
0.9

Kazakhstan
25.7

Ecuador
2

Increasing

Stable

Decreasing

Laos
0.8

Egypt
81.4

Central America
11.4

140

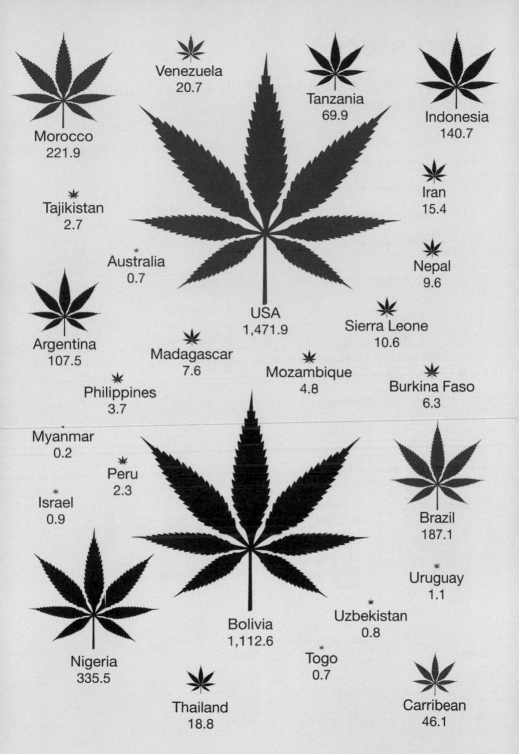

Venezuela
20.7

Tanzania
69.9

Morocco
221.9

Indonesia
140.7

Iran
15.4

Tajikistan
2.7

Australia
0.7

Nepal
9.6

USA
1,471.9

Sierra Leone
10.6

Argentina
107.5

Madagascar
7.6

Mozambique
4.8

Burkina Faso
6.3

Philippines
3.7

Myanmar
0.2

Peru
2.3

Brazil
187.1

Israel
0.9

Uruguay
1.1

Uzbekistan
0.8

Bolivia
1,112.6

Nigeria
335.5

Togo
0.7

Thailand
18.8

Carribean
46.1

Euro stars

Ranking of Michelin-starred restaurants by city in Europe in 2012

Key — **Restaurants with**
- ✿✿✿ 3 Michelin stars
- ✿✿ 2 Michelin stars
- ✿ 1 Michelin star

London
- ✿✿✿ 2
- ✿✿ 7
- ✿ 46

Amsterdam
- ✿✿ 2
- ✿ 9

Paris
- ✿✿✿ 10
- ✿✿ 16
- ✿ 56

Bordeaux
- ✿✿ 1
- ✿ 10

Lyon
- ✿✿✿ 1
- ✿✿ 4
- ✿ 9

Cannes/Antibes
- ✿✿ 3
- ✿ 7

Barcelona
- ✿✿ 2
- ✿ 16

San Sebastian
- ✿✿✿ 3
- ✿✿ 1
- ✿ 4

Madrid
- ✿✿ 6
- ✿ 3

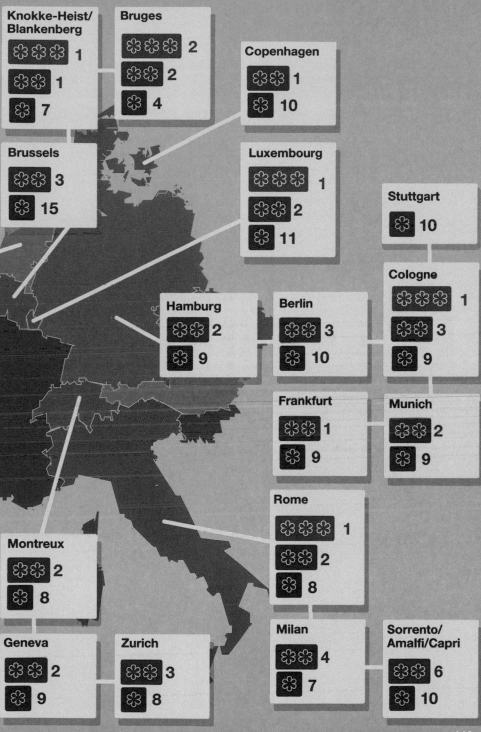

Knokke-Heist/Blankenberg
✱✱✱ 1
✱✱ 1
✱ 7

Bruges
✱✱✱ 2
✱✱ 2
✱ 4

Copenhagen
✱✱ 1
✱ 10

Brussels
✱✱ 3
✱ 15

Luxembourg
✱✱✱ 1
✱✱ 2
✱ 11

Stuttgart
✱ 10

Hamburg
✱✱ 2
✱ 9

Berlin
✱✱ 3
✱ 10

Cologne
✱✱✱ 1
✱✱ 3
✱ 9

Frankfurt
✱✱ 1
✱ 9

Munich
✱✱ 2
✱ 9

Rome
✱✱✱ 1
✱✱ 2
✱ 8

Montreux
✱✱ 2
✱ 8

Milan
✱✱ 4
✱ 7

Sorrento/Amalfi/Capri
✱✱ 6
✱ 10

Geneva
✱✱ 2
✱ 9

Zurich
✱✱ 3
✱ 8

Culture vultures

**The top ten art exhibitions worldwide
in 2011 by daily number of visitors**

The Magical World of Escher
Centro Cultural Banco do Brasil,
Rio de Janeiro

9,677

Kukai's World:
the Arts of Esoteric Buddhism
Tokyo National Museum, Tokyo

9,108

Photoquai
Musée du Quai Branly, Paris

7,304

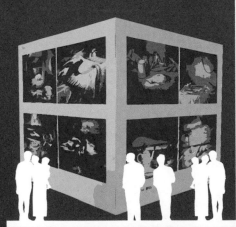

Mariko Mori: Oneness
Centro Cultural Banco do Brasil,
Rio de Janeiro

6,991

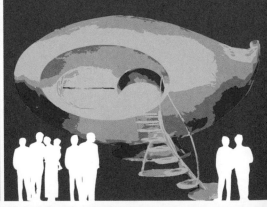

EXIT THROUGH THE GIFT STORE

Landscape Reunited
National Palace Museum, Taipei

8,828

Alexander McQueen: Savage Beauty
Metropolitan Museum of Art, New York

8,025

Claude Monet (1840–1926)
Grand Palais, Paris

7,609

Monumenta: Anish Kapoor
Grand Palais, Paris

6,967

Laurie Anderson
Centro Cultural Banco do Brasil, Rio de Janeiro

6,934

The Prado Museum at the Hermitage
State Hermitage Museum, St Petersburg

6,649

The play's the thing

The largest Shakespeare roles by number of lines

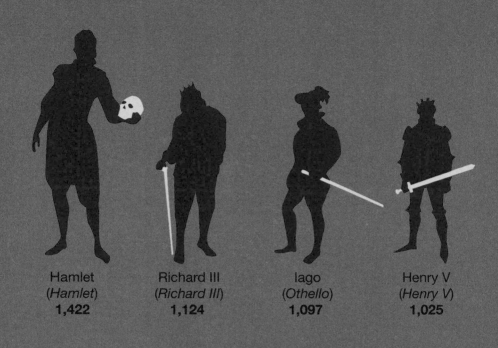

Hamlet
(*Hamlet*)
1,422

Richard III
(*Richard III*)
1,124

Iago
(*Othello*)
1,097

Henry V
(*Henry V*)
1,025

Othello
(*Othello*)
860

Vincentio
(*Measure for Measure*)
820

Coriolanus
(*Coriolanus*)
809

Timon
(*Timon of Athens*)
795

Antony
(*Antony and
Cleopatra*)
766

Richard II
(*Richard II*)
753

Brutus
(*Julius Caesar*)
701

Lear
(*King Lear*)
697

Titus
(*Titus Andronicus*)
687

Macbeth
(*Macbeth*)
681

Rosalind
(*As You Like It*)
668

Leontes
(*The Winter's Tale*)
648

Cleopatra
(*Antony and
Cleopatra*)
622

Prospero
(*The Tempest*)
603

Falstaff
(*Henry IV
Part 2*)
593

Pericles
(*Pericles*)
592

Berowne
(*Love's
Labour's Lost*)
591

Romeo
(*Romeo and
Juliet*)
591

Falstaff
(*Henry IV
Part 1*)
585

Portia
(*The Merchant
of Venice*)
565

147

WLTM?

Online dating in the USA

 Mail | **Key statistics**

54 million
Number of single people in the USA

40 million
Number of people in the USA who have tried online dating

$1.049 billion
Annual revenue from the online dating industry

$239
Average spent by each dating site customer per year

Average length of courtship for marriages (months)

Met online | Met offline
18.5 | 42

What's most important on a first date

♥ ♥ ♥ 30% Personality
♡ ♥ ♥ 23% Smile & looks
♡ ♡ ♥ 14% Sense of humor
♡ ♡ ♥ 10% Career & education

64% say common interests are the most important factor

49% say physical characteristics are the most important factor

Online dating users

52.4%
Male

47.6%
Female

Men prefer	Women prefer
The career girl—**42%**	**38%**—Nice guy
The girl next door—**34%**	**34%**—Mix of nice/bad boy
The hot girl—**24%**	**15%**—Bad boy

71% of people believe in love at first sight

53% of people say they dated more than one person simultaneously

Most attractive hair color

- **32%** Blonde
- **16%** Brown
- **16%** Black
- **16%** Don't mind
- **8%** Red
- **8%** Bald
- **4%** Gray

Online dating facts

A woman's desirablility online peaks at the age of 21

At age 26, women have more online admirers than men

By age 48, men have twice as many online admirers as women

Men lie most about: age, height, income

Women lie most about: weight, physical build, age

Two wheels good

Landmark bicycle designs

Celerifere
Comte Mede de Sivrac, 1791

Macmillan Velocipede
Macmillan Kirkpatrick, 1839

Boneshaker
Pierre and Ernest Michaux, 1863

Penny Farthing
James Starley, 1870

Safety bicycle
H. J. Lawson, 1873

Rover safety bicycle
John Kemp Starley, 1885

Challand Velocipede
M. Challand, 1897

Three-speed bicycle
Raleigh, 1909

Elgin Bluebird
Elgin Bluebird, 1935

Everest Racer
Everest, 1949

Shelby Donald Duck
Shelby, 1949

Huffy Radio Cycle
Huffy, 1955

Moulton Continental
Moulton, 1962

Schwin Sting Ray
Schwin, 1964

Raleigh Record
Raleigh, 1967

Raleigh Chopper
Raleigh, 1968

Raleigh Folder
Raleigh, 1971

Specialized Stumpjumer
Specialized, 1981

Lotus 108
Lotus Engineering, 1990

Track changes

Countries with the biggest increase—and those with the greatest decrease—in length of railroad track since the 1997 Kyoto Protocol, which required governments to reduce greenhouse gases to 1990 levels. One major strategy to comply with this was to increase rail travel

Argentina — 6,667.3 miles / 10,730km
Germany — 2,947 miles / 4,744km
Poland — 1,566 miles / 2,521km
Indonesia — 1,214 miles / 1,954km
Colombia — 920 miles / 1,482km
Russia — 910 miles / 1,466km
Chile — 789 miles / 1,271km
D.R. Congo — 690 miles / 1,111km
Uganda — 615 miles / 991km
Greece — 590 miles / 951km

Key

Reduction in track length miles / km

Increase in track length miles / km

Algeria: 466 miles / 750km

Italy: 576 miles / 928km

Iran: 969 miles / 1,560km

South Africa: 1,862km / 1,156 miles

France: 1,257 miles / 2,024km

Spain: 1,708 miles / 2,749km

China: 4,324 miles / 7,925km

Brazil: 15,928 miles / 25,634km

Canada: 21,508 miles / 34,614km

USA: 38,368 miles / 61,748km

Dancing shoes

Basic steps of Latin American dances

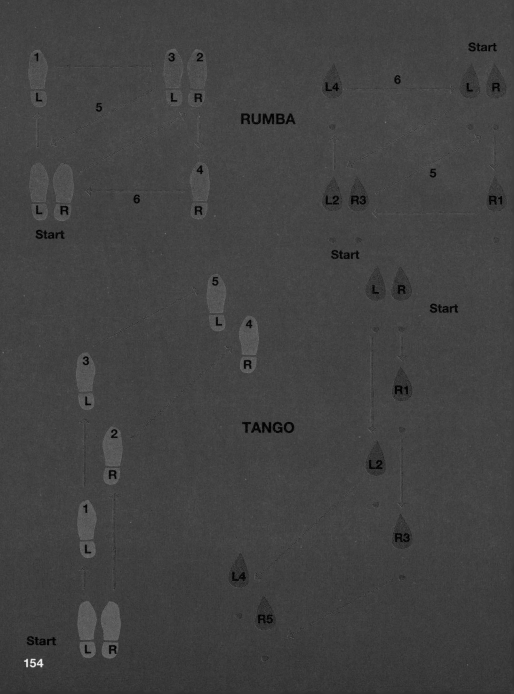

RUMBA

TANGO

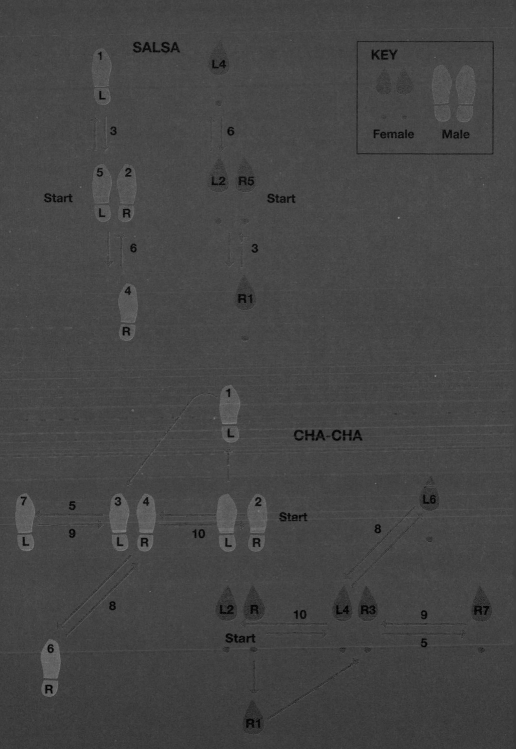

SALSA

KEY

Female   Male

CHA-CHA

Money makes the world go around

Average monthly wages around the world (USD)

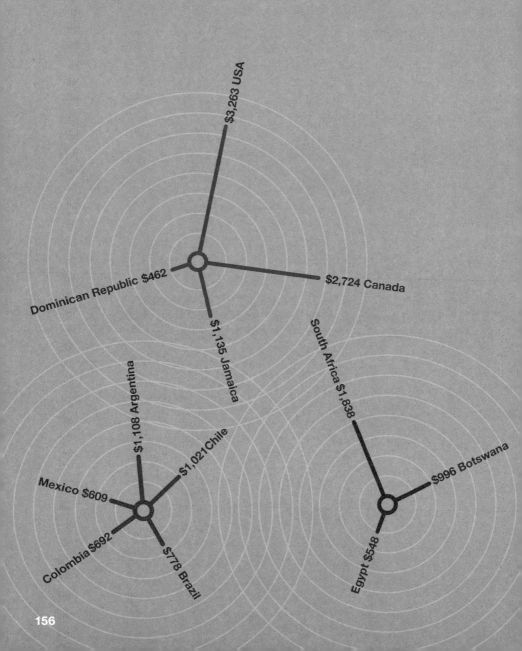

$3,263 USA

$2,724 Canada

Dominican Republic $462

$1,135 Jamaica

South Africa $1,838

$1,108 Argentina

$1,021 Chile

Mexico $609

$996 Botswana

Colombia $692

$778 Brazil

Egypt $548

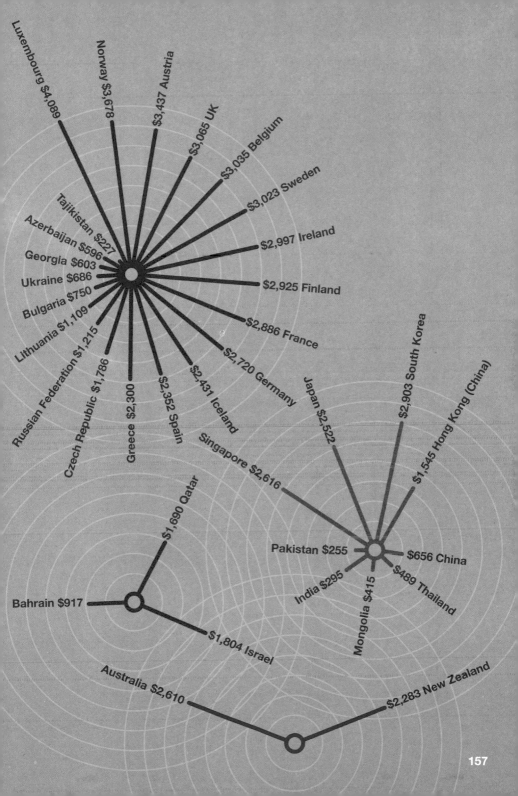

Luxembourg $4,089
Norway $3,678
$3,437 Austria
$3,065 UK
$3,035 Belgium
$3,023 Sweden
$2,997 Ireland
$2,925 Finland
$2,886 France
$2,720 Germany
$2,431 Iceland
$2,352 Spain
Greece $2,300
Czech Republic $1,786
Russian Federation $1,215
Lithuania $1,109
Bulgaria $750
Ukraine $686
Georgia $603
Azerbaijan $596
Tajikistan $227

Japan $2,522
$2,903 South Korea
$1,545 Hong Kong (China)
Singapore $2,616
Pakistan $255
$656 China
India $295
Mongolia $415
$489 Thailand

$1,690 Qatar
Bahrain $917
$1,804 Israel
Australia $2,610
$2,283 New Zealand

CERN nation

Proportion of funding provided by member nations to CERN (Conseil Européenne pour la Recherche Nucléaire or European Organization for Nuclear Research)

Countries of origin of resident physicists
Russia: 826
CIS (Former soviet republics): 71
Eastern Europe: 129
Canada: 150
USA: 1,685
Latin America: 136
Japan: 203
China: 83
India: 93
Israel: 60
Other: 350

Germany 19.44% (213.2m CHF)

France 15.42% (167.1m CHF)

UK 15% (164.6m CHF)

Figures shown are Swiss Francs (CHF)

Bulgaria 0.32% (3.5m CHF)

Slovakia 0.55% (6.0m CHF)

Hungary 0.67% (7.4m CHF)

Czech Republic 1.13% (12.4m CHF)

Portugal 1.26% (13.8m CHF)

Finland 1.26% (13.9m CHF)

Denmark 1.79% (19.7m CHF)

Greece 1.9% (20.1m CHF)

Austria 2.18% (23.9m CHF)

Sweden 2.46% (27.0m CHF)

Norway 2.61% (28.6m CHF)

Belgium 2.78% (30.5m CHF)

Poland 3.15% (34.5m CHF)

Switzerland 3.79% (41.6m CHF)

Netherlands 4.28% (47.0m CHF)

Spain 8.82% (96.8m CHF)

Italy 11.19% (122.8m CHF)

Bald facts

The different patterns of age-related male pattern baldness as defined by the Norwood scale

Type I
Minimal hair loss

Type II
Limited areas of recession of the hair line at the temples

Type IV
Sparse hair or no hair on the back of the head

Type V
Less distinct gap between hair loss at the front and back

Type III
First sign of real
pattern baldness

Type III vertex
Hair loss from the back
of the head and with limited
hair line recession

Type VI
No bridge of hair crossing the
crown. Areas of hair loss at the
front and back joined together

Type VII
The most severe
form of hair loss

Jewels and the crown

The regalia used in the coronation of the British monarch

St Edward's Staff

St Edward's crown is used to crown the monarch by the Archbishop of Canterbury

The Scepter of the Dove represents the Holy Ghost and the qualities of equity and mercy

Imperial State Crown has 2,868 diamonds, 273 pearls, 17 sapphires, 11 emeralds

The Sovereign's Scepter with cross represents the monarch's temporal power under God

The Orb symbolizes Christ's dominion over Earth

162

The Sword
of State

The Jeweled Sword of Offering
is presented to the monarch by
the Archbishop to symbolize
the fact that royal power is at
the service of the church

The Sword of
Spiritual Justice

The Sword of Mercy's
blade is short and
square to symbolize
the virtue of mercy of
the sovereign

The Sword of
Temporal Justice

The Spurs, which are not worn,
are there to represent knightly chivalry,
and the Armills or bracelets represent
sincerity and wisdom. A new pair
of gold Armills was presented to
the Queen by the Commonwealth
for the 1953 coronation

The Ampulla is used to anoint
the monarch with holy oil

163

Biggest bangs

The volcanic eruptions of the 20th century that produced the greatest volume of debris—boulders, stones, and ash— compared to the volume of stone (in cubic meters) used in the construction of the Great Pyramid at Giza

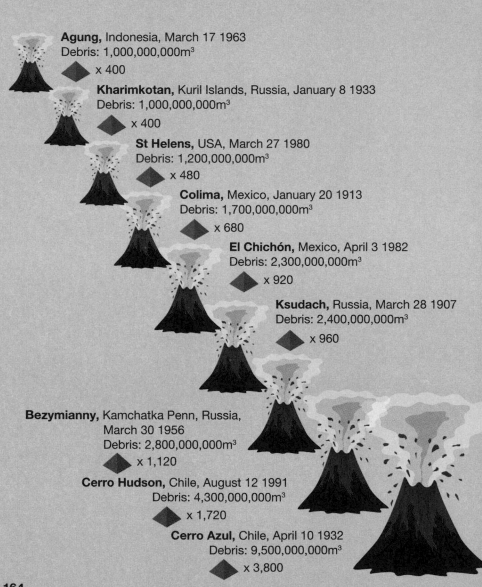

Agung, Indonesia, March 17 1963
Debris: 1,000,000,000m³
x 400

Kharimkotan, Kuril Islands, Russia, January 8 1933
Debris: 1,000,000,000m³
x 400

St Helens, USA, March 27 1980
Debris: 1,200,000,000m³
x 480

Colima, Mexico, January 20 1913
Debris: 1,700,000,000m³
x 680

El Chichón, Mexico, April 3 1982
Debris: 2,300,000,000m³
x 920

Ksudach, Russia, March 28 1907
Debris: 2,400,000,000m³
x 960

Bezymianny, Kamchatka Penn, Russia, March 30 1956
Debris: 2,800,000,000m³
x 1,120

Cerro Hudson, Chile, August 12 1991
Debris: 4,300,000,000m³
x 1,720

Cerro Azul, Chile, April 10 1932
Debris: 9,500,000,000m³
x 3,800

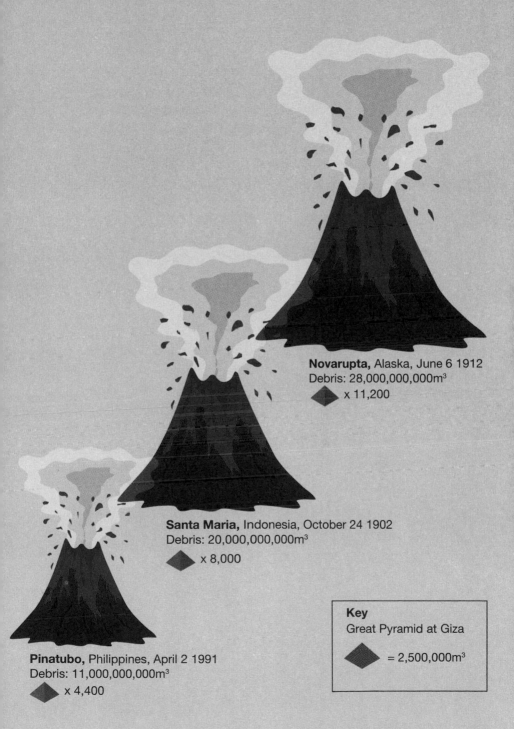

Novarupta, Alaska, June 6 1912
Debris: 28,000,000,000m³
x 11,200

Santa Maria, Indonesia, October 24 1902
Debris: 20,000,000,000m³
x 8,000

Pinatubo, Philippines, April 2 1991
Debris: 11,000,000,000m³
x 4,400

Key
Great Pyramid at Giza

= 2,500,000m³

165

Water world

Water supply versus population worldwide

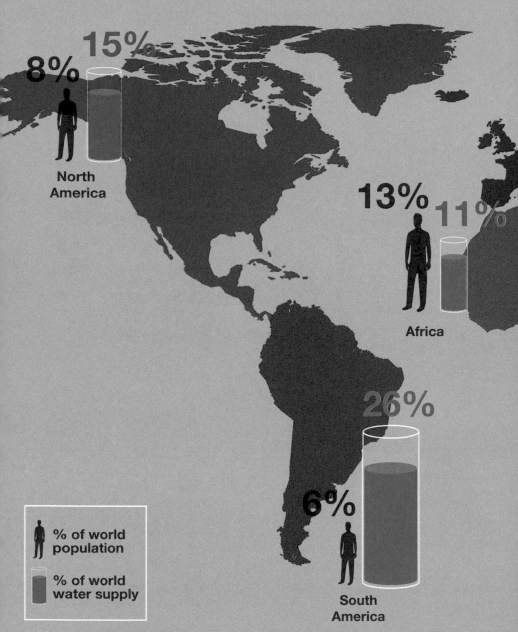

8% 15%
North America

13% 11%
Africa

26% 6%
South America

% of world population

% of world water supply

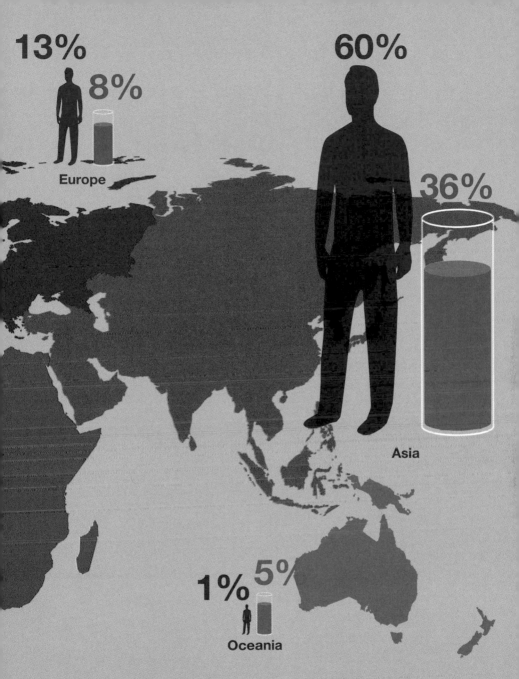

13%

8%

Europe

60%

36%

Asia

1% 5%

Oceania

Carefree

The least stressful jobs in the USA

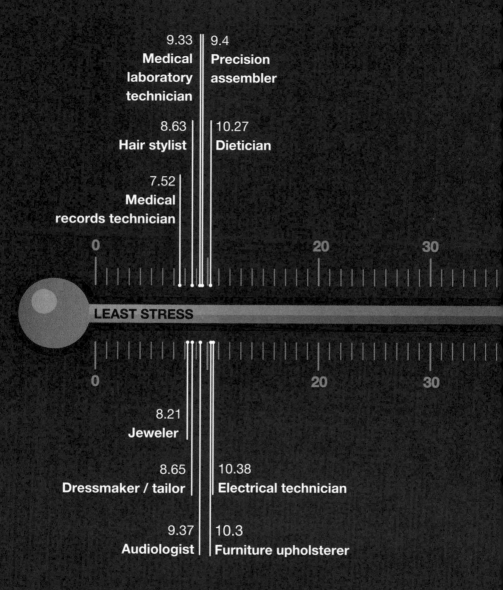

9.33
Medical laboratory technician

9.4
Precision assembler

8.63
Hair stylist

10.27
Dietician

7.52
Medical records technician

0   20   30

LEAST STRESS

0   20   30

8.21
Jeweler

8.65
Dressmaker / tailor

10.38
Electrical technician

9.37
Audiologist

10.3
Furniture upholsterer

The most stressful jobs in the USA

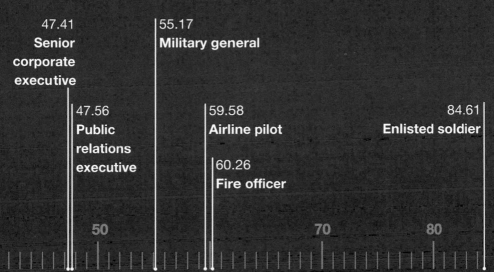

47.41
Senior corporate executive

55.17
Military general

47.56
Public relations executive

59.58
Airline pilot

60.26
Fire officer

84.61
Enlisted soldier

50   70   80

MOST STRESS

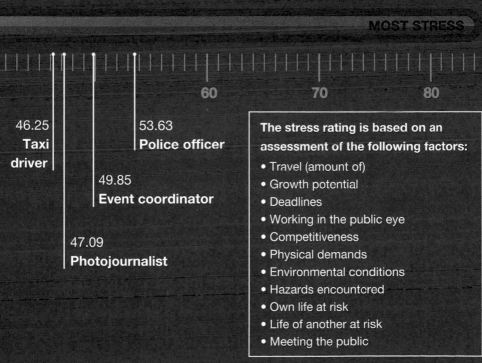

60   70   80

46.25
Taxi driver

53.63
Police officer

49.85
Event coordinator

47.09
Photojournalist

The stress rating is based on an assessment of the following factors:
- Travel (amount of)
- Growth potential
- Deadlines
- Working in the public eye
- Competitiveness
- Physical demands
- Environmental conditions
- Hazards encountered
- Own life at risk
- Life of another at risk
- Meeting the public

Bed heads

Countries with the most hospital beds per 100,000 population

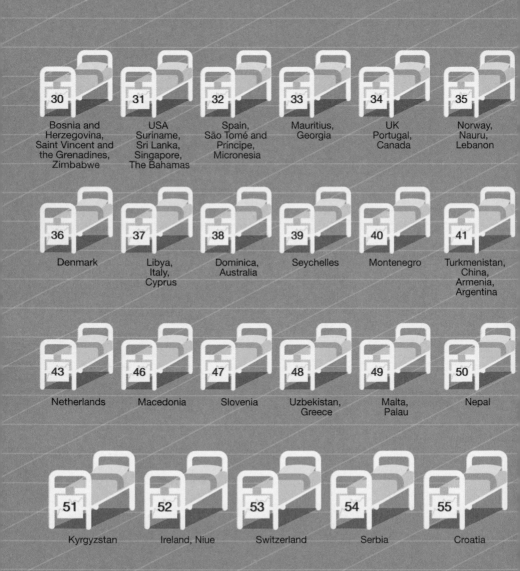

30 Bosnia and Herzegovina, Saint Vincent and the Grenadines, Zimbabwe

31 USA Suriname, Sri Lanka, Singapore, The Bahamas

32 Spain, São Tomé and Príncipe, Micronesia

33 Mauritius, Georgia

34 UK Portugal, Canada

35 Norway, Nauru, Lebanon

36 Denmark

37 Libya, Italy, Cyprus

38 Dominica, Australia

39 Seychelles

40 Montenegro

41 Turkmenistan, China, Armenia, Argentina

43 Netherlands

46 Macedonia

47 Slovenia

48 Uzbekistan, Greece

49 Malta, Palau

50 Nepal

51 Kyrgyzstan

52 Ireland, Niue

53 Switzerland

54 Serbia

55 Croatia

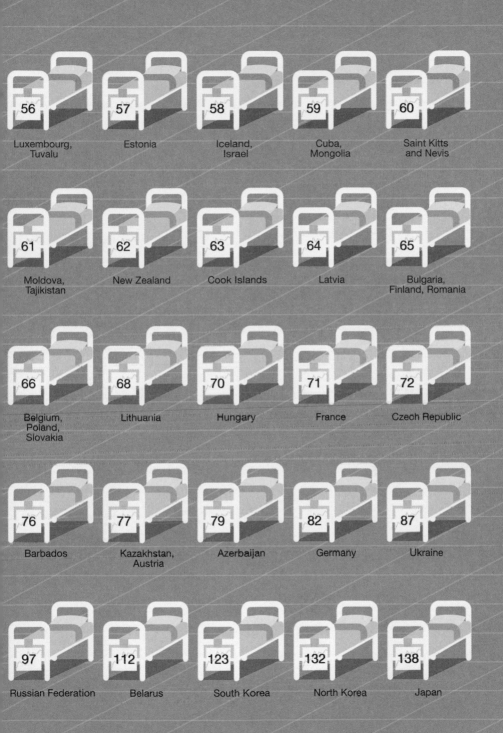

56 Luxembourg, Tuvalu

57 Estonia

58 Iceland, Israel

59 Cuba, Mongolia

60 Saint Kitts and Nevis

61 Moldova, Tajikistan

62 New Zealand

63 Cook Islands

64 Latvia

65 Bulgaria, Finland, Romania

66 Belgium, Poland, Slovakia

68 Lithuania

70 Hungary

71 France

72 Czech Republic

76 Barbados

77 Kazakhstan, Austria

79 Azerbaijan

82 Germany

87 Ukraine

97 Russian Federation

112 Belarus

123 South Korea

132 North Korea

138 Japan

Payback time

The UK expenses scandal broke in 2009 after a British newspaper leaked details of the expenses claims of members of parliament. As a result of the investigation, the following MPs had the largest amount of money to pay back to the UK taxpayer

The Bank PLC
00 00 00
Date 01-01-00
Pay UK Taxpayers Only
£ 42,458.21
Barbara Follett
Labour

00 00 00
Date 01-01-00
Pay UK Taxpayers Only
£ 36,250.00
Bernard Jenkin
Conservatives

The Bank PLC
Date 01-01-00
Pay UK Taxpayers Only
£ 31,193,00
Andrew MacKay
Conservatives

00 00 00
Date 01-01-00
Pay UK Taxpayers Only
£ 29,691.93
David Heathcoat-Amory
Conservatives

The Bank PLC — 00 00 00 — Date 01-01-00
Pay UK Taxpayers Only
£ 29,398.46
John Gummer
Conservatives

The Bank PLC — Date 01-01-00
Pay UK Taxpayers Only
£ 29,243.00
Julie Kirkbride
Conservatives

The Bank PLC — 00 00 00 — Date 01-01-00
Pay UK Taxpayers Only
£ 24,878.27
Liam Fox
Conservatives

The Bank PLC — 00 00 00 — Date 01-01-00
Pay UK Taxpayers Only
£ 20,639.42
Douglas Hogg
Conservatives

The Bank PLC — 00 00 00 — Date 01-01-00
Pay UK Taxpayers Only
£ 19,169.56
Alun Michael
Labour

The Bank PLC — 00 00 00 — Date 01-01-00
Pay UK Taxpayers Only
£ 17,364.76
Jonathan Djanogly
Conservatives

173

Now boarding

The world's 20 shortest nonstop scheduled passenger routes by distance traveled

 DEPARTURES

ROUTE	DISTANCE (miles / km)
Westray to Papa Westray	1.7 miles / 2.7km
Ipota to Dillons Bay	4.1 miles / 6.6km
Warraber Island to Yam Island	6.1 miles / 9.8km
St. Kitts to Nevis	9 miles / 14km
Hoolehua to Kalaupapa	9 miles / 14km
Saipan to Tinian	10.8 miles / 17.4km
Papeete (Faaa) to Moorea	11 miles / 18km
Connemara to Aran Islands	11.5 miles / 18.5km
Block Island to Westerly	14.8 miles / 23.8km
Nadi to Malololailai	15.5 miles / 24.9km
Brazzaville to Kinshasa	16 miles / 26km
Cayman Brac to Little Cayman	17.2 miles / 27.7km
Skagway to Haines	17.8 miles / 28.6km
Karpathos to Kasos Island	18.6 miles / 29.9km
Guernsey to Alderney	20 miles / 32km
Kirkenes to Vadsø	24 miles / 38.6km
Taitung to Green Island	24 miles / 38.6km
Grand Turk to Salt Cay	24.2 miles / 38.9km
Moscow, Idaho, to Lewiston	25 miles / 40km
Saint-Pierre to Miquelon	25 miles / 40km

DURATION	COUNTRY	AIRLINE
02 min	UK	Loganair
10 min	Vanuatu	Air Vanuatu
15 min	Australia	Regional Pacific
05 min	St Kitts and Nevis	LIAT
10 min	Hawaii, USA	Pacific Wings
10 min	Northern Mariana Islands	Freedom Air (Guam)
15 min	Tahiti	Air Tahiti
10 min	Ireland	Aer Arann
15 min	USA	New England Airlines
10 min	Fiji	Air Pacific
20 min	D.R. Congo	Hewa Bora Airways
10 min	Cayman Islands	Cayman Airways
15 min	USA	Wings of Alaska
15 min	Greece	Olympic Airways
12 min	UK	Aurigny
15 min	Norway	Widerøe
15 min	Taiwan	Daily Air
10 min	Turks and Caicos Islands	SkyKing
25 min	USA	Horizon Air
15 min	Martinique	Air Saint-Pierre

Banana equivalent dose

Bananas contain a small amount of radioactive isotopes. There is a system of measuring the absorption of radiation from different sources called the "banana equivalent dose." Eating 80 million bananas would constitute a fatal dose of radiation. Here are some others on the scale:

Value	Description
1	Eating a banana
50	Dental X-ray
200	Chest X-ray
300	Yearly release target for a nuclear power plant
400	Flight from London to New York
1,000	Approximate total dose received at Fukushima Town Hall in two weeks following 2011 nuclear accident
4,000	Mammogram
40,000	10 years of normal background dose, 85% of which is from natural sources
70,000	CT scan

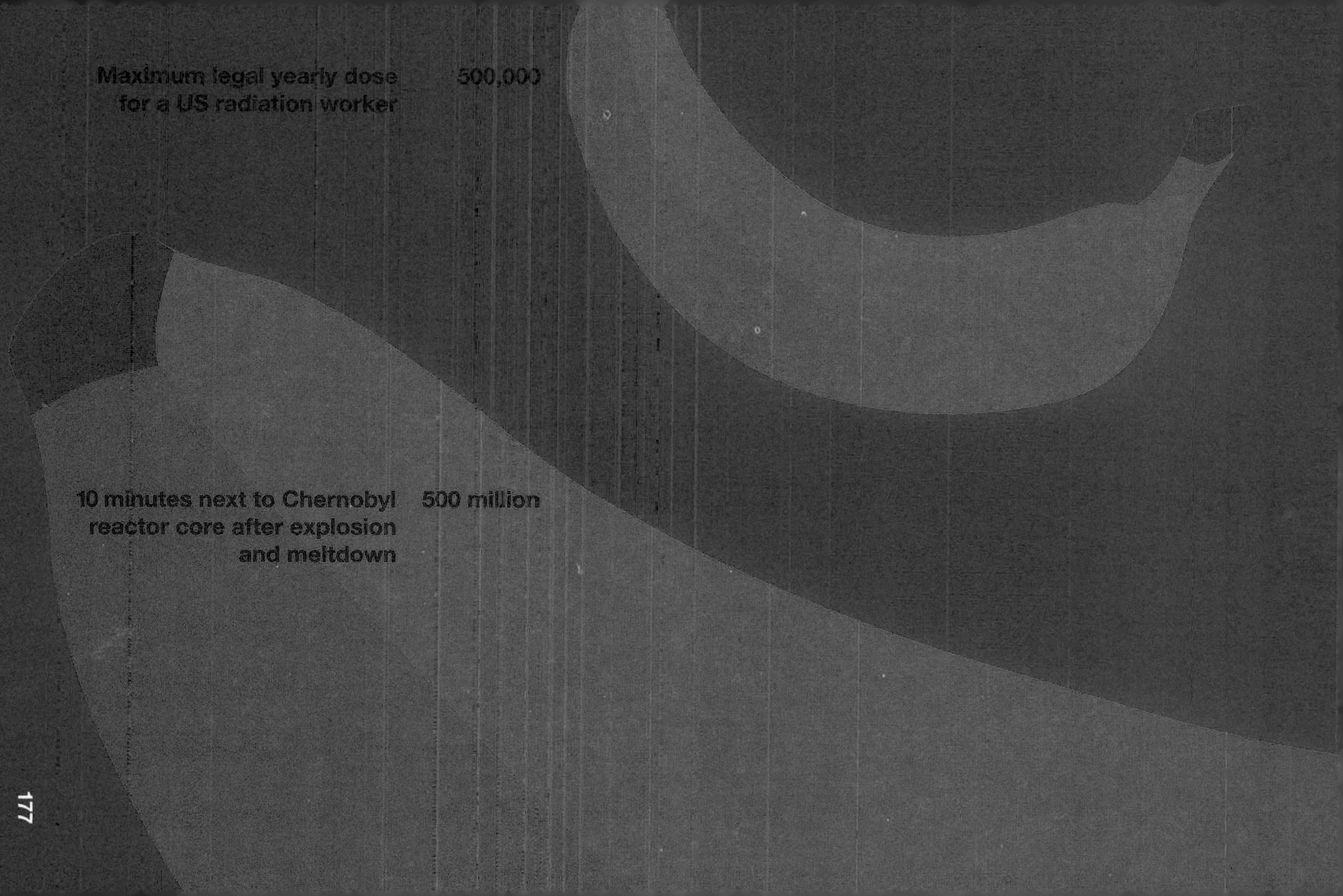

Maximum legal yearly dose
for a US radiation worker

300,000

10 minutes next to Chernobyl
reactor core after explosion
and meltdown

500 million

To boldly go . . .

The duration of unmanned space probe missions

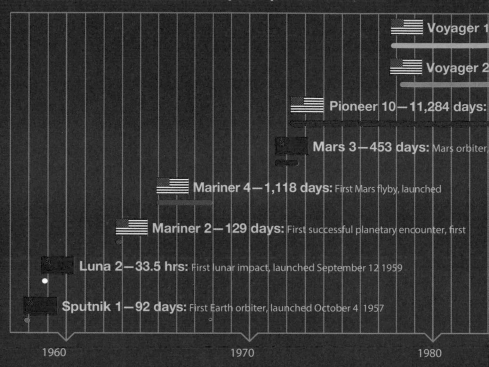

Voyager 1

Voyager 2

Pioneer 10—11,284 days:

Mars 3—453 days: Mars orbiter,

Mariner 4—1,118 days: First Mars flyby, launched

Mariner 2—129 days: First successful planetary encounter, first

Luna 2—33.5 hrs: First lunar impact, launched September 12 1959

Sputnik 1—92 days: First Earth orbiter, launched October 4 1957

1960   1970   1980

Mission destinations

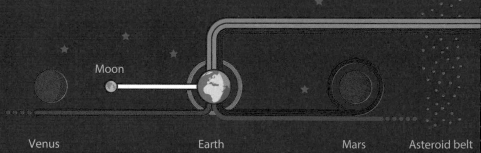

Moon

Venus   Earth   Mars   Asteroid belt

13,267 days: Jupiter and Saturn flyby, furthest human-made object, launched September 5 1977

13,283 days: Jupiter, Saturn, first Uranus, and Neptune flyby, launched August 20 1977

First Jupiter flyby, launched March 3 1972

first Mars lander, first Mars atmospheric probe, launched May 28 1971

November 28 1964

successful Venus flyby, launched August 27 1962

1990   2000   2010

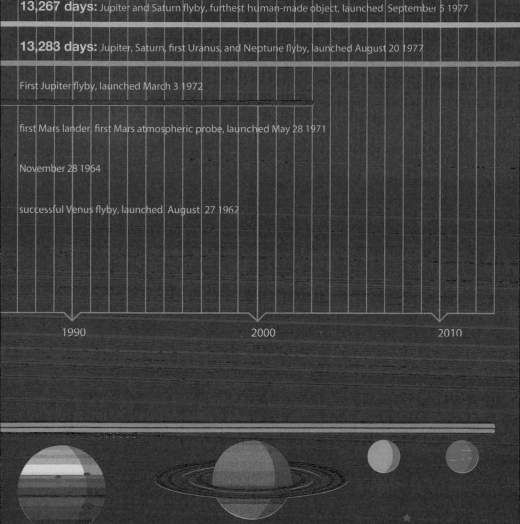

Peaches and Cream Day

A selection of US national food days

JANUARY
2 Cream Puff Day
3 Chocolate-Covered Cherry Day
4 Spaghetti Day
5 Whipped Cream Day
20 Cheese Lover's Day
21 Granola Bar Day
23 Pie Day
25 Irish Coffee Day
31 Popcorn Day

FEBRUARY
1 Baked Alaska Day
3 Carrot Cake Day
11 Peppermint Patty Day
12 Plum Pudding Day
20 Cherry Pie Day
21 Sticky Bun Day
25 Clam Chowder Day
26 Pistachio Day
27 Chocolate Cake Day

MARCH
2 Banana Cream Pie Day
4 Poundcake Day
6 Frozen Food Day
12 Baked Scallops Day
13 Coconut Torte Day
14 Potato Chip Day
20 Ravioli Day
24 Chocolate-Covered Raisins Day
26 Waffle Day

APRIL
2 Peanut Butter and Jelly Day
3 Chocolate Mousse Day
6 Caramel Popcorn Day
7 Coffee Cake Day
11 Cheese Fondue Day
15 Glazed Ham Day
16 Baked Ham with Pineapple Day
17 Cheeseball Day
29 Shrimp Scampi Day

MAY
8 Coconut Cream Pie Day
12 Nutty Fudge Day
13 Apple Pie Day
18 Cheese Souffle Day
19 Devil's Food Cake Day
20 Quiche Lorraine Day
22 Vanilla Pudding Day
26 Blueberry Cheesecake Day

JUNE
2 Rocky Road Day
3 Donut Day (1st weekend in June)
5 National Gingerbread Day
16 Fudge Day
17 Apple Strudel Day
17 Cherry Tart Day
21 Peaches and Cream Day

JULY

- 5 Apple Turnover Day
- 6 Fried Chicken Day
- 12 Pecan Pie Day
- 20 Ice Cream Day
- 20 Lollipop Day
- 21 Creme Brulee Day
- 25 Hot Fudge Sundae Day
- 28 Hamburger Day
- 30 Cheesecake Day

AUGUST

- 2 Ice Cream Sandwich Day
- 2 Ice Cream Soda Day
- 6 Root Beer Float Day
- 15 Lemon Meringue Pie Day
- 17 Vanilla Custard Day
- 18 Ice Cream Pie Day
- 25 Banana Split Day
- 26 Cherry Popsicle Day
- 30 Toasted Marshmallow Day

SEPTEMBER

- 5 Cheese Pizza Day
- 12 Chocolate Milkshake Day
- 14 Cream-Filled Donut Day
- 19 Butterscotch Pudding Day
- 28 Strawberry Cream Pie Day

OCTOBER

- 4 Taco Day
- 5 Apple Betty Day
- 10 Angel Food Cake Day
- 11 Sausage Pizza Day
- 18 Chocolate Cupcake Day
- 20 Brandied Fruit Day
- 22 Nut Day
- 23 Boston Cream Pie Day

NOVEMBER

- 2 Deviled Egg Day
- 4 Candy Day
- 6 Nachos Day
- 7 Bittersweet Chocolate with Almonds Day
- 10 Vanilla Cupcake Day
- 27 Bavarian Cream Pie Day
- 30 Mousse Day

DECEMBER

- 4 Cookie Day
- 6 Gazpacho Day
- 7 Cotton Candy Day
- 9 Brownie Day
- 14 Bouillabaisse Day
- 15 Lemon Cupcake Day
- 18 Roast Suckling Pig Day
- 24 Egg Nog Day
- 25 Pumpkin Pie Day

Women in power

Countries with the lowest and highest percentage of women members of parliament. Where there are two legislative chambers the numbers are added together

Parliaments with lowest percentage of women

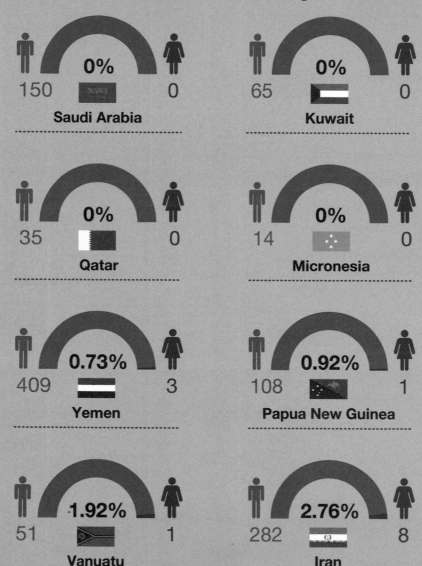

0%
150 · Saudi Arabia · 0

0%
65 · Kuwait · 0

0%
35 · Qatar · 0

0%
14 · Micronesia · 0

0.73%
409 · Yemen · 3

0.92%
108 · Papua New Guinea · 1

1.92%
51 · Vanuatu · 1

2.76%
282 · Iran · 8

Parliaments with highest percentage of women

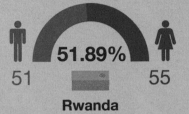

51 **51.89%** 55

Rwanda

14 **50%** 14

Andorra

321 **45.22%** 265

Cuba

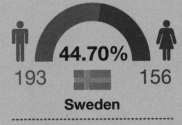

193 **44.70%** 156

Sweden

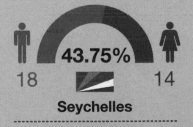

18 **43.75%** 14

Seychelles

115 **42.50%** 85

Finland

55 **40.22%** 37

Nicaragua

38 **39.68%** 25

Iceland

I spy satellites

Number of satellites in orbit around the earth by country

27 India

21 UK

20 Germany

17 Canada

9 Brazil

9 Italy

9 Israel

9 Spain

5 Malaysia

5 Norway

5 South Korea

4 Mexico

3 Pakistan

3 Singapore

3 Thailand

2 Switzerland

1 Denmark

1 Greece

1 Iran

1 Kazakhstan

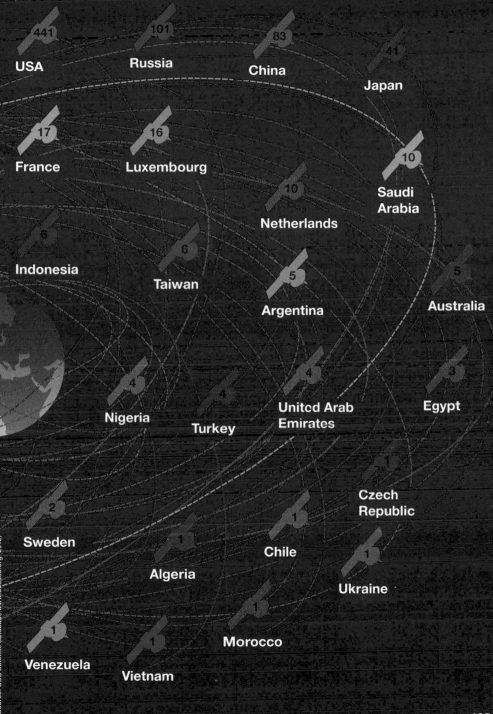

441 USA
101 Russia
83 China
41 Japan
17 France
16 Luxembourg
10 Netherlands
10 Saudi Arabia
6 Indonesia
6 Taiwan
5 Argentina
5 Australia
4 Nigeria
4 Turkey
4 United Arab Emirates
3 Egypt
2 Sweden
1 Algeria
1 Chile
1 Czech Republic
1 Ukraine
1 Venezuela
1 Vietnam
1 Morocco

Source: UCS Satellite database www.ucsusa.org (2012)

Goal!

Referee signals to indicate a score in different sports

Rugby union

"Try scored"

Raise 1 hand above the head with back to dead-ball line

Cricket

"6 scored"

Raise both hands above the head

Rugby league

"Try scored"

Point to the place where the try is scored with extended arm and flat open hand

Field hockey

"Goal scored"

Point both arms horizontally to the center of the field

Soccer

"Goal scored"

Point your arm level at the center circle of the pitch

Basketball

"3-point shot"

Raise both hands above the head with 3 fingers showing on both hands

American football

"Touchdown"

Raise both hands above the head

Volleyball

"Point scored"

Hold up the index finger of 1 hand —left or right depending on which side has won the point

Ice hockey

"Goal scored"

Point to the net

Water polo

"Goal scored"

Point to the center of the pool

The price of love

The world's most expensive weddings (USD)

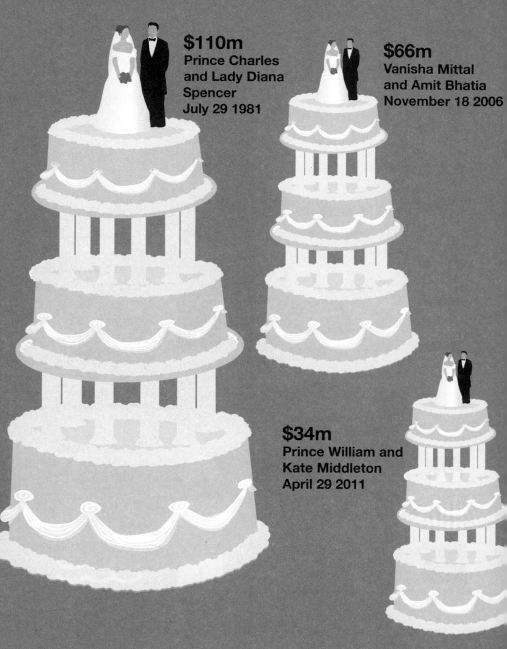

$110m
Prince Charles
and Lady Diana
Spencer
July 29 1981

$66m
Vanisha Mittal
and Amit Bhatia
November 18 2006

$34m
Prince William and
Kate Middleton
April 29 2011

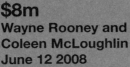

$8m
Wayne Rooney and
Coleen McLoughlin
June 12 2008

$5m
Chelsea Clinton and
Marc Mezvinsky
July 31 2010

$4.2m
Liza Minnelli
and David Gest
March 16 2002

$4m
Elizabeth Taylor
and Larry Fortensky
October 6 1991

$3.6m
Paul McCartney
and Heather Mills
June 11 2002

$2.6m
Elizabeth Hurley
and Arun Nayar
March 2 2007

$2.2m
Christina Aguilera
and Jordan Bratman
November 19 2005

$2.2m
Tom Cruise and
Katie Holmes
November 18 2006

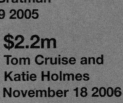

$1.6m
Catherine Zeta-Jones
and Michael Douglas
November 18 2000

189

Bearded felons

Percentage of bearded criminals from different countries on Interpol's wanted list

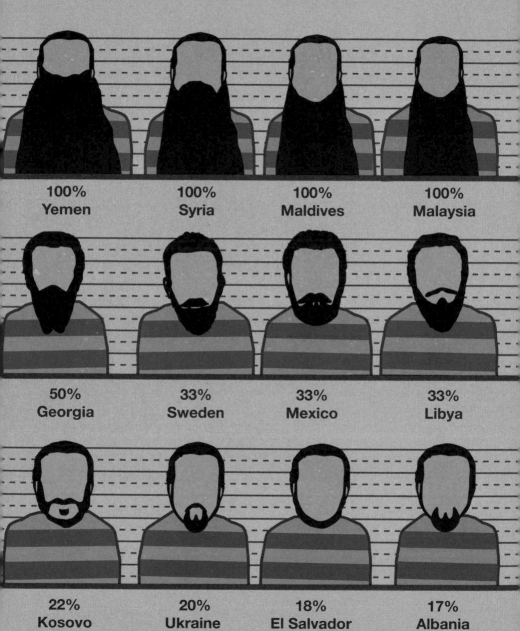

100%
Yemen

100%
Syria

100%
Maldives

100%
Malaysia

50%
Georgia

33%
Sweden

33%
Mexico

33%
Libya

22%
Kosovo

20%
Ukraine

18%
El Salvador

17%
Albania

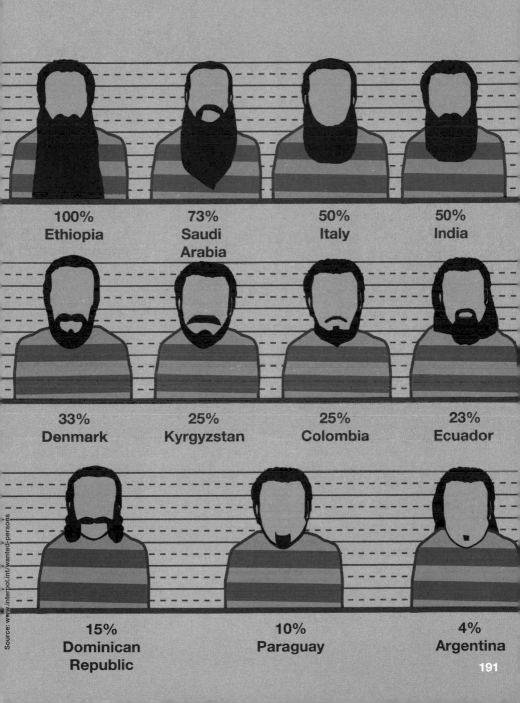

100% Ethiopia

73% Saudi Arabia

50% Italy

50% India

33% Denmark

25% Kyrgyzstan

25% Colombia

23% Ecuador

15% Dominican Republic

10% Paraguay

4% Argentina

Source: www.interpol.int/wanted-persons

Chance hands

The odds of being dealt different hands
in 5-card poker

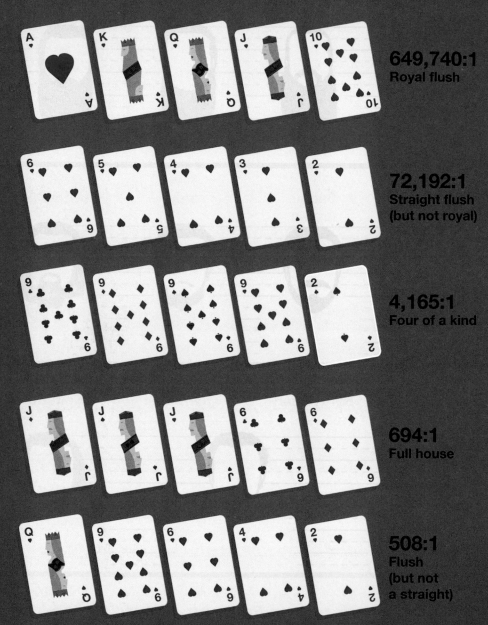

649,740:1
Royal flush

72,192:1
Straight flush
(but not royal)

4,165:1
Four of a kind

694:1
Full house

508:1
Flush
(but not
a straight)

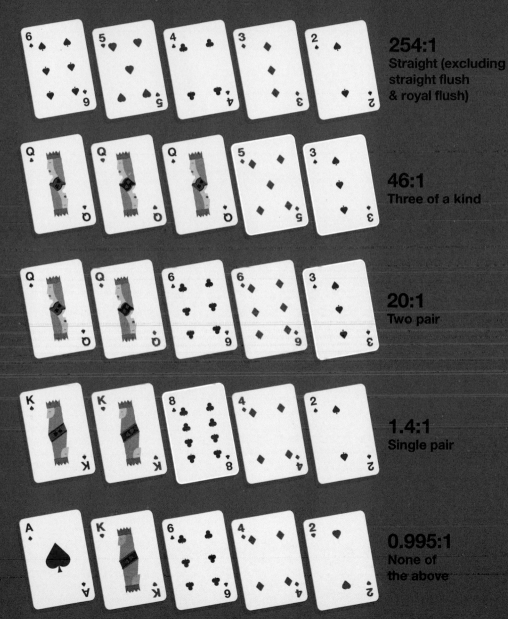

254:1
Straight (excluding straight flush & royal flush)

46:1
Three of a kind

20:1
Two pair

1.4:1
Single pair

0.995:1
None of the above

Glastonbury

Facts and figures from the world's best-known music festival

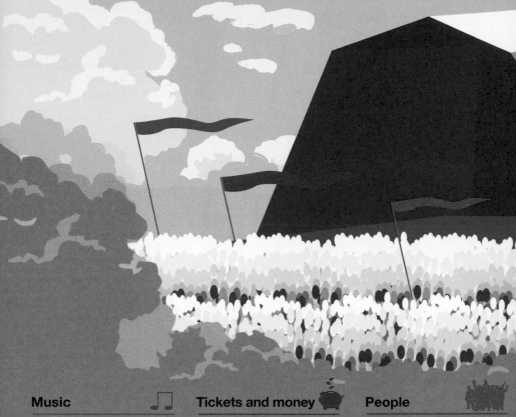

Music ♫

2,000 performances on over 50 stages in 4 days

T. Rex were the first headliners at the Worthy Farm festival in 1970, replacing The Kinks at short notice

Tickets and money

Entry:
1970—$1.55 / £1
1979—$8 / £5
1987—$33 / £21
1990—$59 / £38
2000—$135 / £87
2011—$302 / £195

Glastonbury contributes around $127m / £82m to the UK economy

$309m / £2m was donated to good causes in 2009 including WaterAid, Oxfam, and Greenpeace

People

250,000 was the biggest crowd in 2000

8.6 million viewers watched the BBC's Glastonbury coverage in 2011. 2.6 million BBC viewers watched Beyoncé

500 doctors, nurses, ambulance crews, and an intensive care unit, treat about 3,000 people over the weekend. Several babies have been born at the festival

Infrastructure

900 acres (345ha) of site—
more than 1.5 miles (2.5km)
across, with a perimeter of
about 8.5 miles (13.5km)

6 bridges

37 miles (80km) of fencing

800 stalls for traders selling
food, drink, clothes, and
other goods and services

Garbage

2 million-liter
subterranean reservoirs

4,700 toilets

1,000 people are involved
in clearing trash, filling
12,000 oil drums, 4,000 can
banks, and 160 skips—all
of which are redecorated
every year

1,650 tons of waste left
behind in 2009, half of which
was recycled

Weather

5 inches of rain fell on
Friday June 18 1982

10,000 pairs of Wellington
boots were sent as an
emergency shipment in
2007

Population explosion

Human population growth from 1 billion (1804) to present

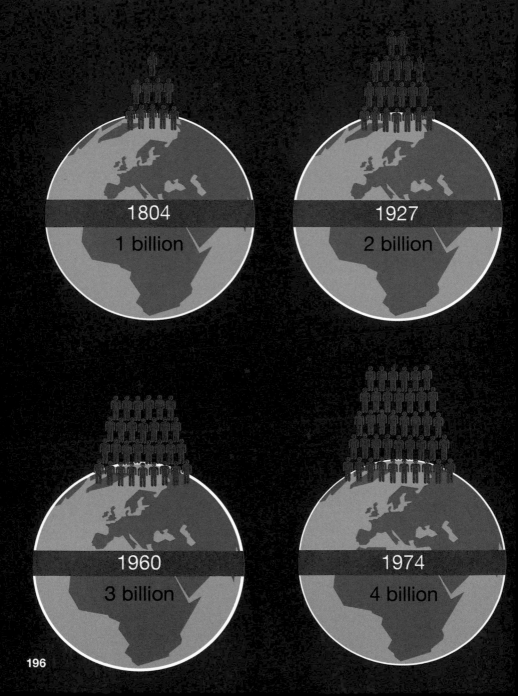

1804
1 billion

1927
2 billion

1960
3 billion

1974
4 billion

=100 million people

1987
5 billion

1999
6 billion

2011
7 billion

A bicycle made for...

City bicycle-sharing schemes ranked by number of bicycles per 1,000 urban population

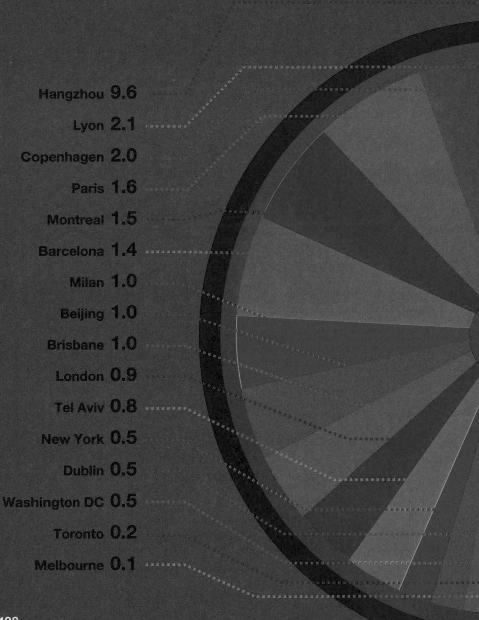

Hangzhou 9.6
Lyon 2.1
Copenhagen 2.0
Paris 1.6
Montreal 1.5
Barcelona 1.4
Milan 1.0
Beijing 1.0
Brisbane 1.0
London 0.9
Tel Aviv 0.8
New York 0.5
Dublin 0.5
Washington DC 0.5
Toronto 0.2
Melbourne 0.1

Bad hair reigns

Facial hair of the great dictators

Saddam Hussein
1937–2006

Ho Chi Minh
1890–1969

Adolf Hitler
1889–1945

Joseph Stalin
1878–1953

Genghis Khan
1162–1227

Enver Pasha
1881–1922

Kaiser Wilhelm II
1859–1941

Muammar Gaddafi
1942–2011

Keeping it brief

Texting abbreviations in different languages

Pq — Spanish
Cz — German
Parske — French
Bcz — English

Because

A2 — Spanish
CU — German
A tt — French
CU — English

See you

Salu2 — Spanish
Hi — German
Lut — French
Hi — English

Hi

Nse — Spanish
Ka — German
NSP — French
Idk — English

I don't know

Tq — Spanish
Ild — German
JTM — French
Ilu/ily — English

I love you

HI — Spanish
L8r — German
A+ — French
L8R — English

Later

Playing tribute

The best-named tribute bands in the world

1 MANDONNA

2 AC/DShe

3 NEARVANA

4 PinkFraud

5 FAKE THAT

6 Björn Again

7 U2-2

1. Madonna 2. AC/DC 3. Nirvana 4. Pink Floyd
5. Take That 6. Abba 7. U2 8. David Bowie

8

9 MUSED

10 COOL PLAY

11 ROLLING THE STONES

12 THE BEATLES

13 CON JOVI

14 LEZ-ZEPPELIN

15 FLEETWOOD MAC

9. Muse   10. Coldplay   11. Rolling Stones   12. The Beatles
13. Bon Jovi   14. Led Zeppelin   15. Fleetwood Mac

World Cup soccer balls

World cup ball models from Uruguay 1930 to South Africa 2010

URUGUAY 1930
Ball model: T-Model
70 goals in 18 games
Goals per game: 3.88

ITALY 1934
Ball model: Federale 102
70 goals in 17 games
Goals per game: 4.12

FRANCE 1938
Ball model: Allen
84 goals in 18 games
Goals per game: 4.67

BRAZIL 1950
Ball model: Super
Duplo T
88 goals in 22 games
Goals per game: 4

SWITZERLAND 1954
Ball model: Swiss World
Champion
140 goals in 26 games
Goals per game: 5.38

SWEDEN 1958
Ball model: Top Star
126 goals in 35 games
Goals per game: 3.6

CHILE 1962
Ball model: Mr Crack
89 goals in 32 games
Goals per game: 2.78

ENGLAND 1966
Ball model: Challenge
4-Star
89 goals in 32 games
Goals per game: 2.78

MEXICO 1970
Ball model: Telstar Durlast
95 goals in 32 games
Goals per game: 2.97

GERMANY 1974
Ball model: Telstar Durlast
97 goals in 38 games
Goals per game: 2.55

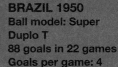